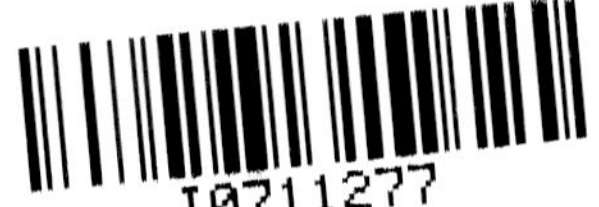

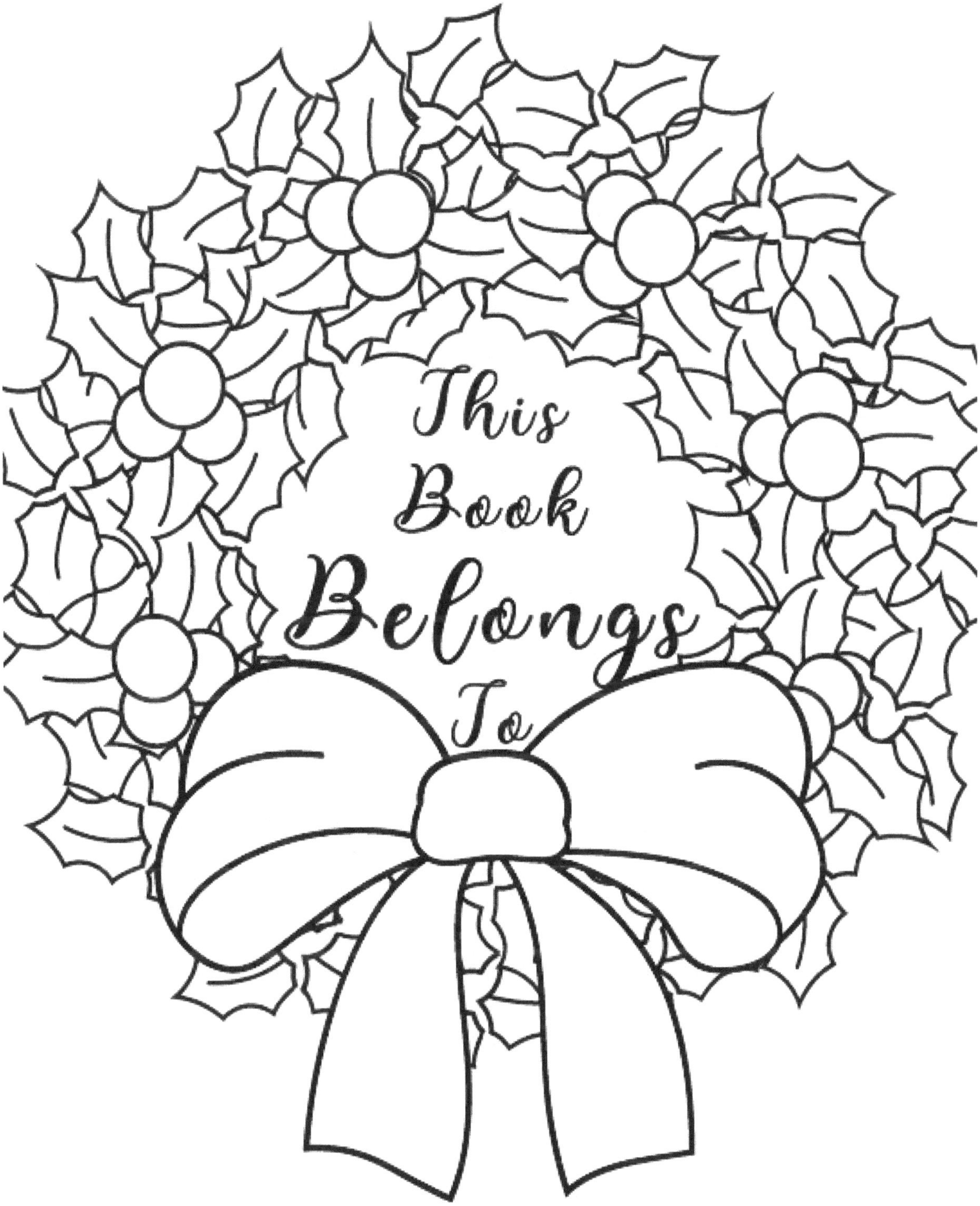

This Book
Belongs
To

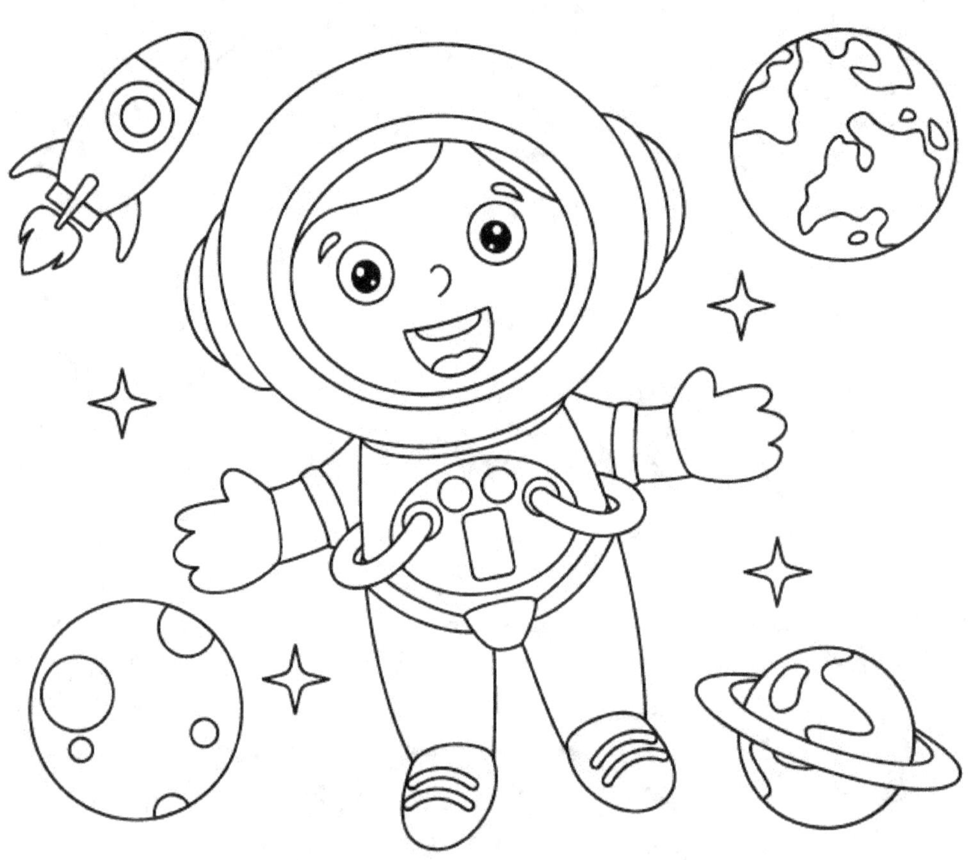

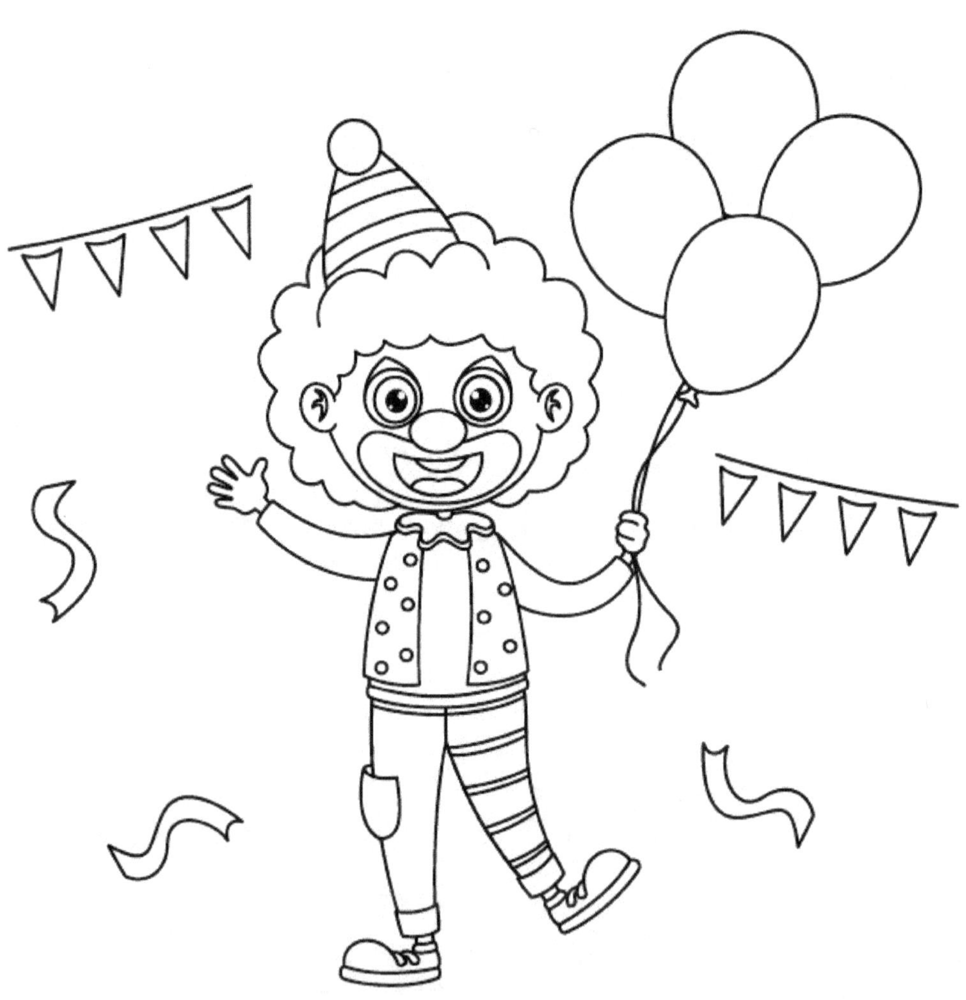

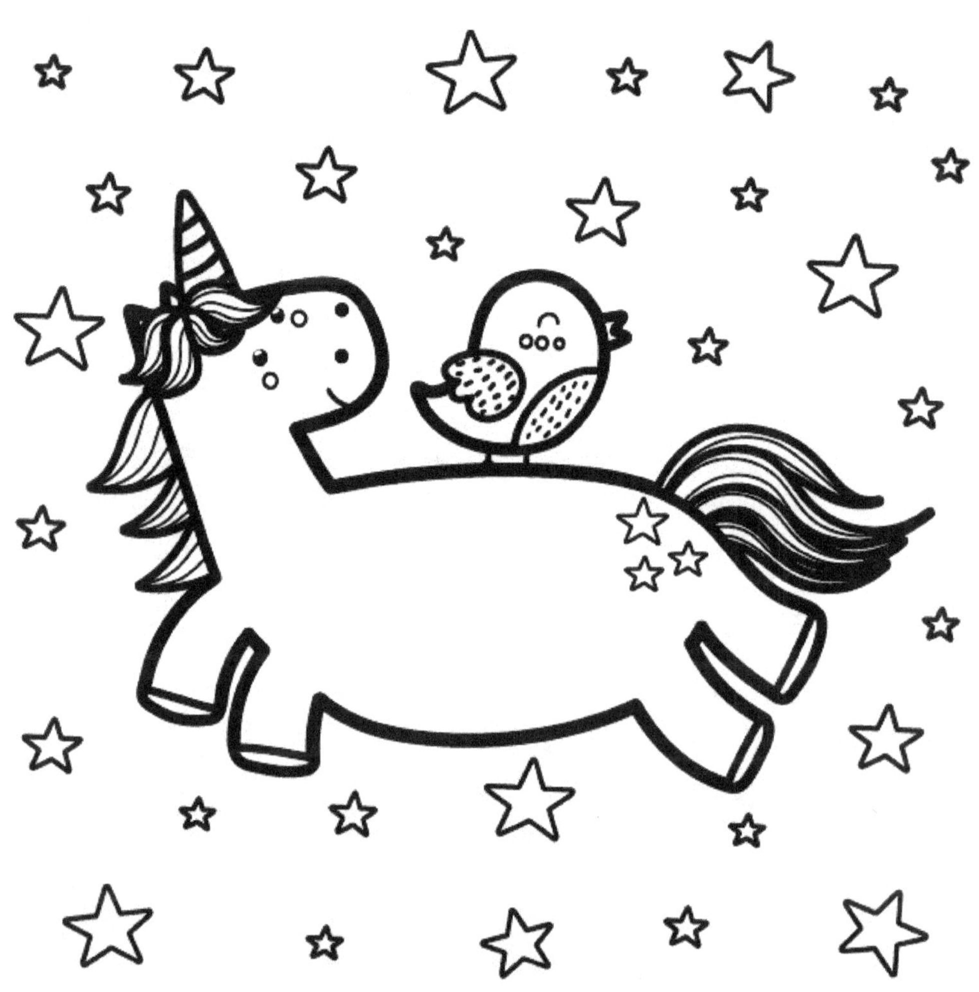

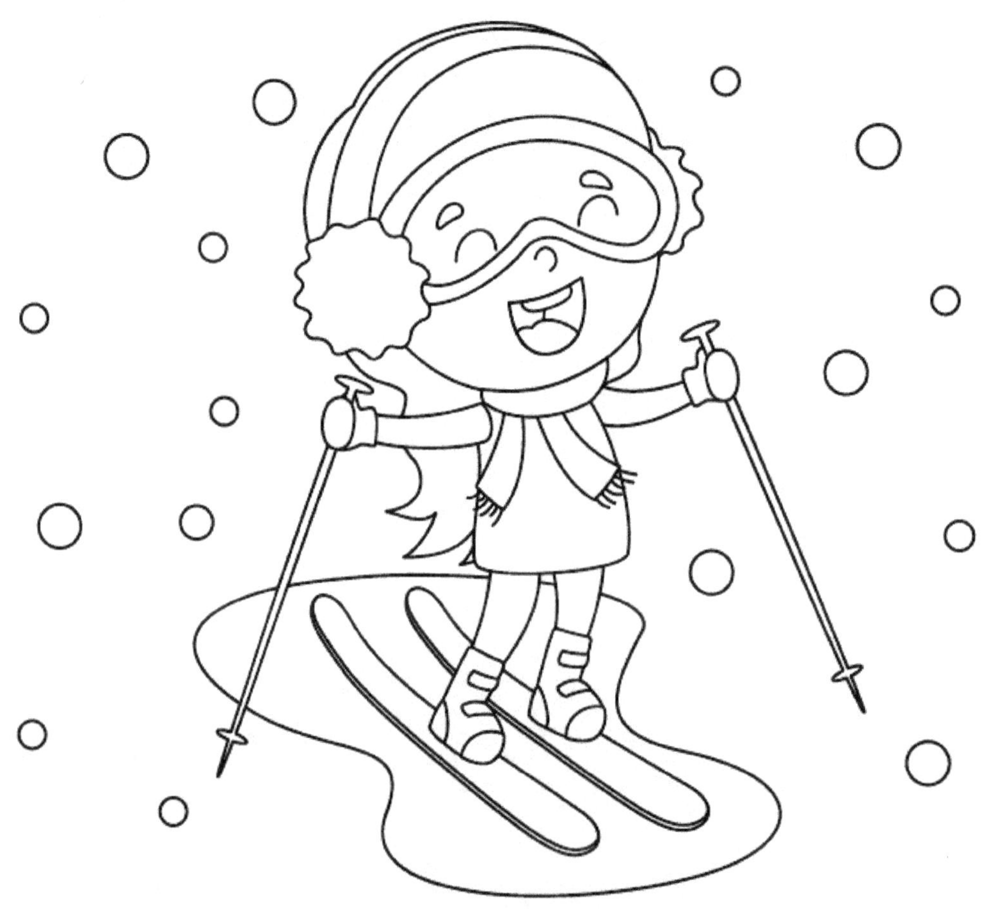

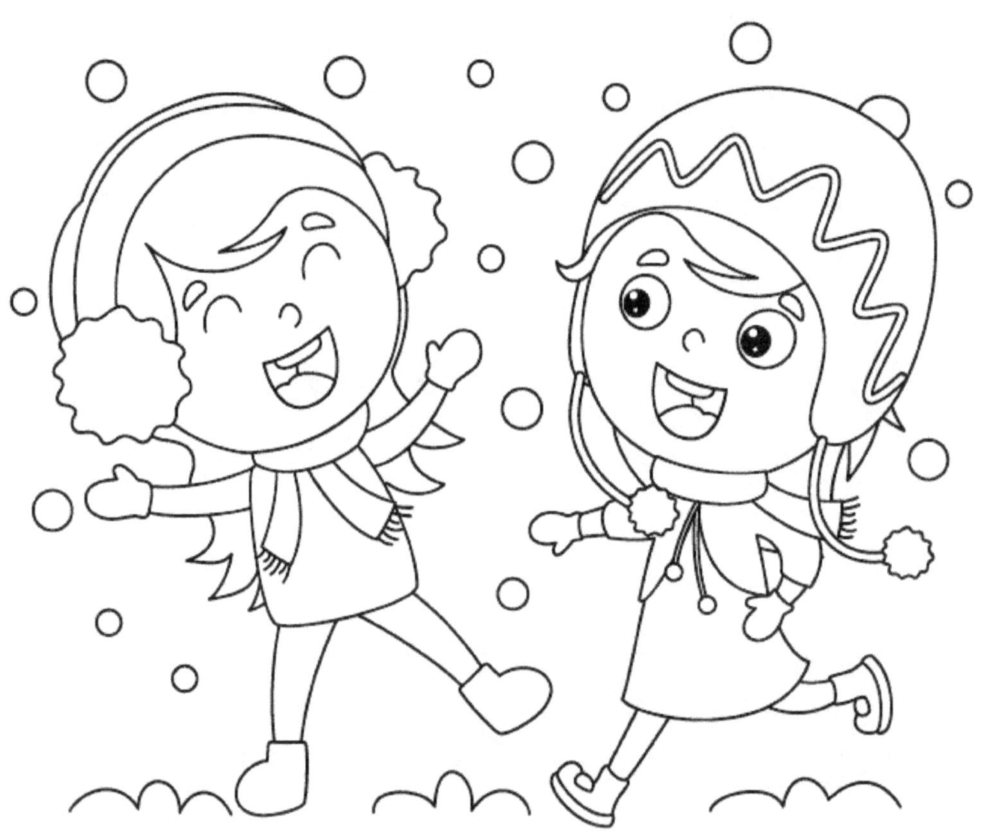

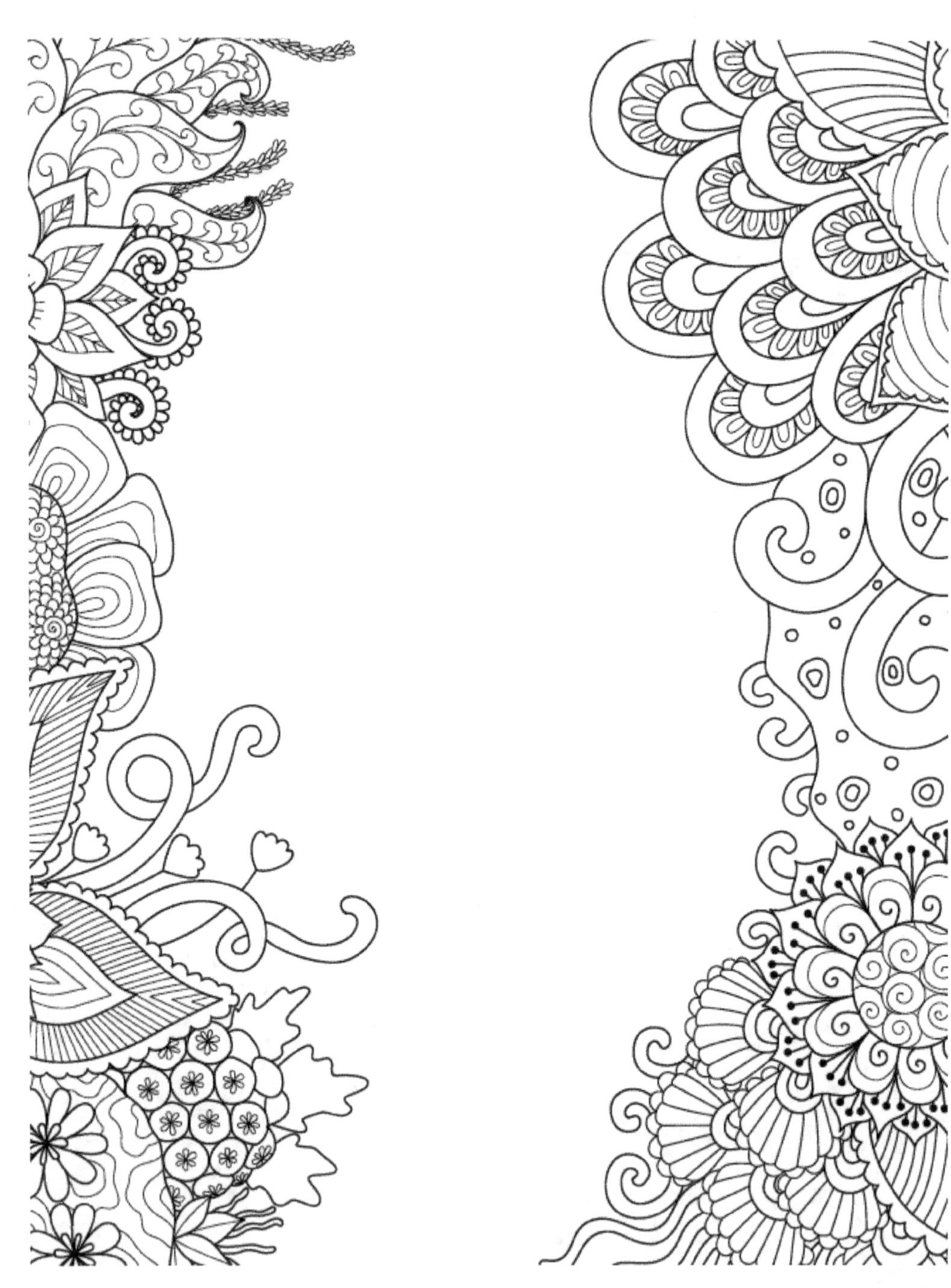

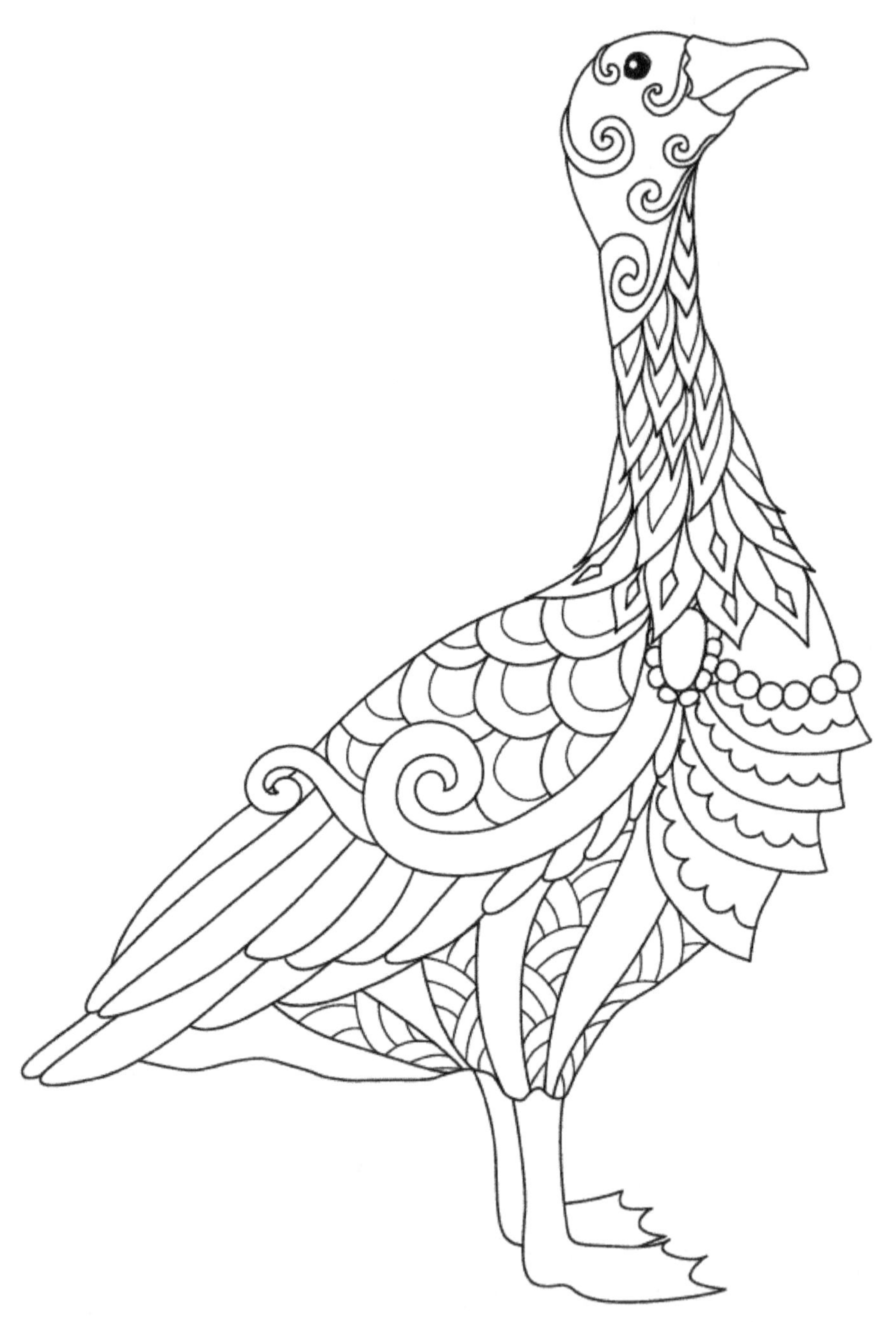

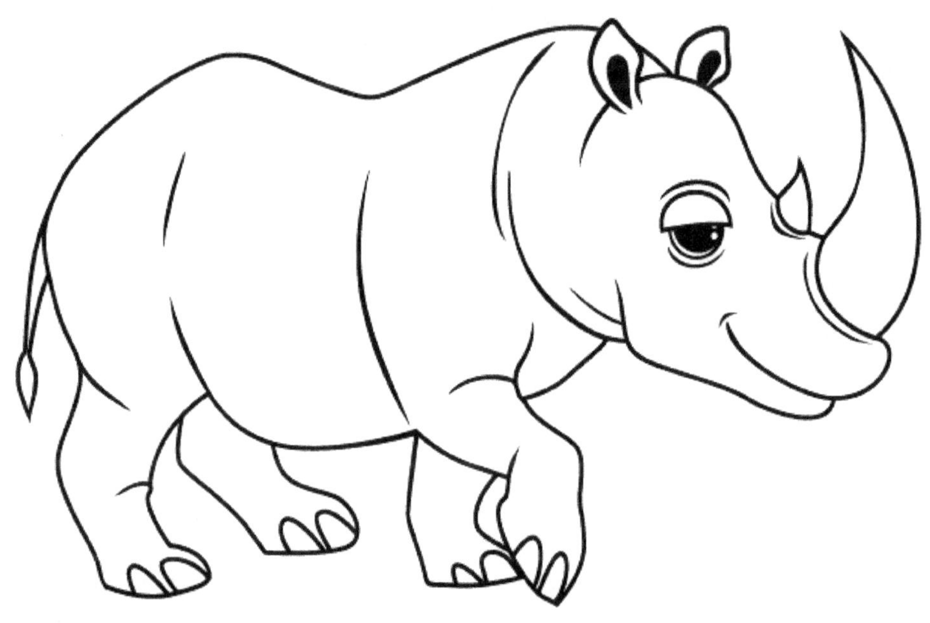

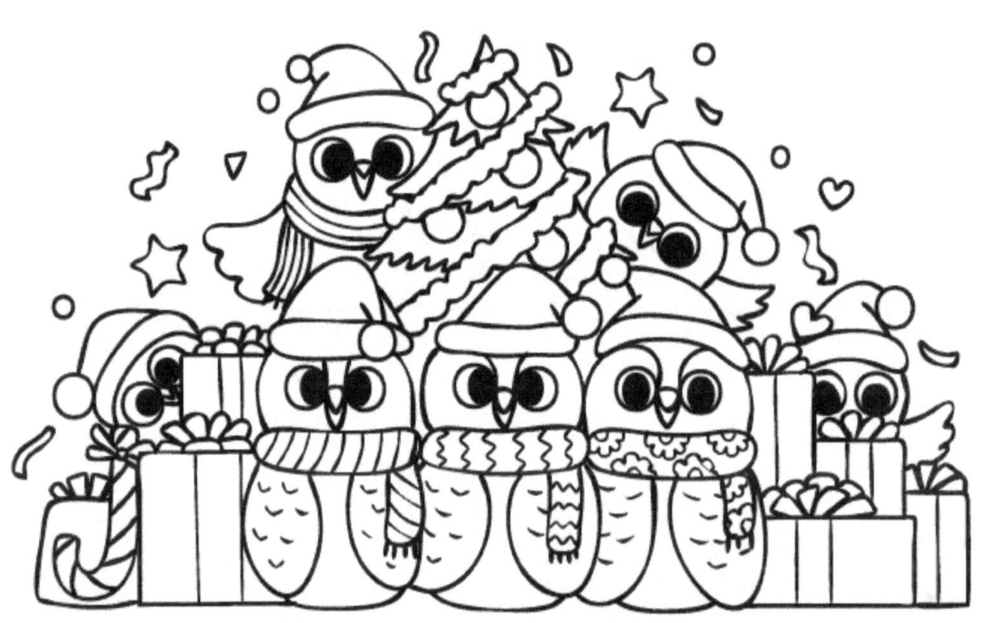

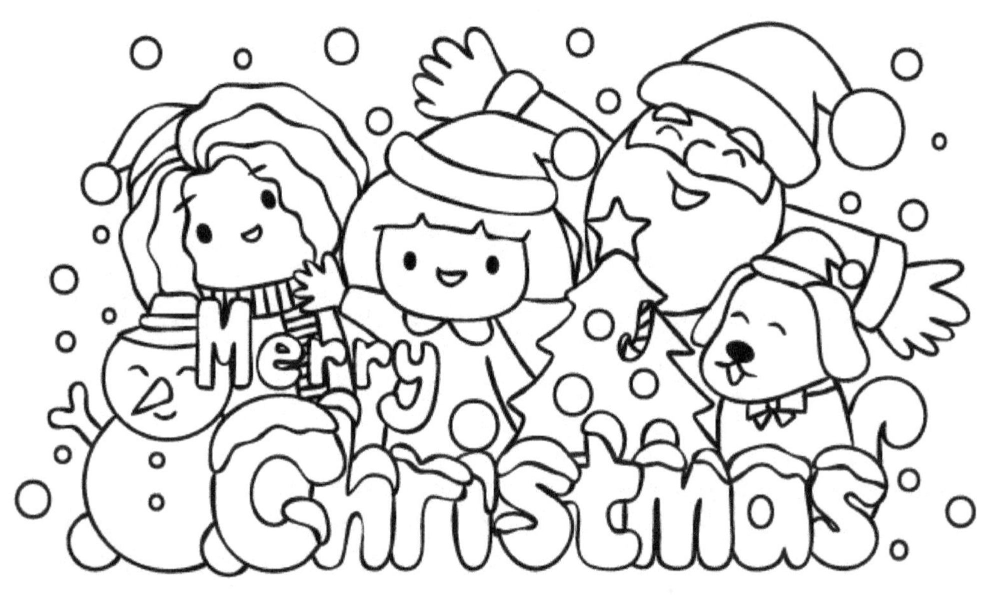

Merry
Christmas

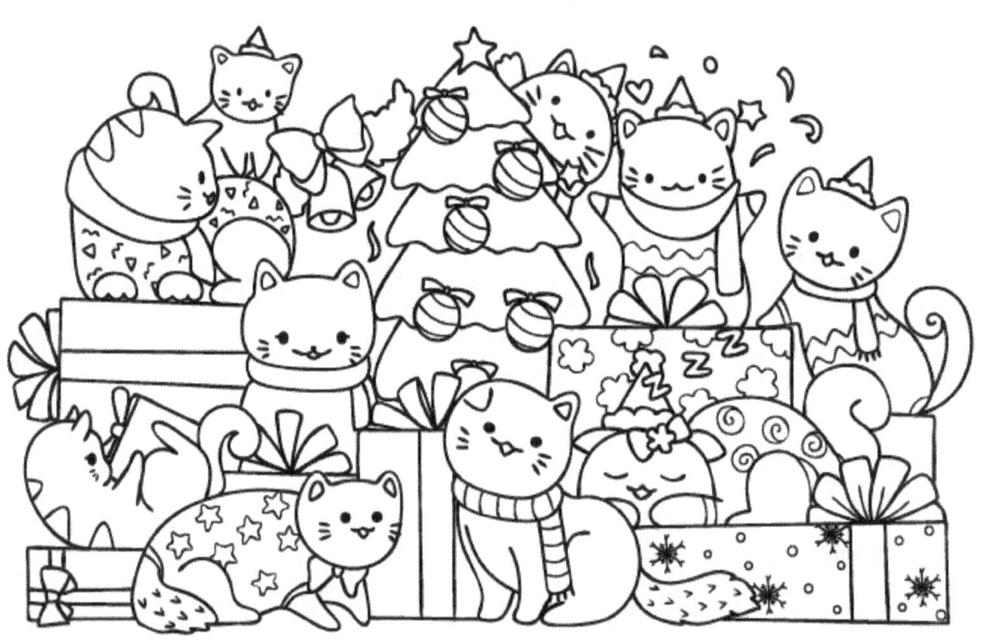

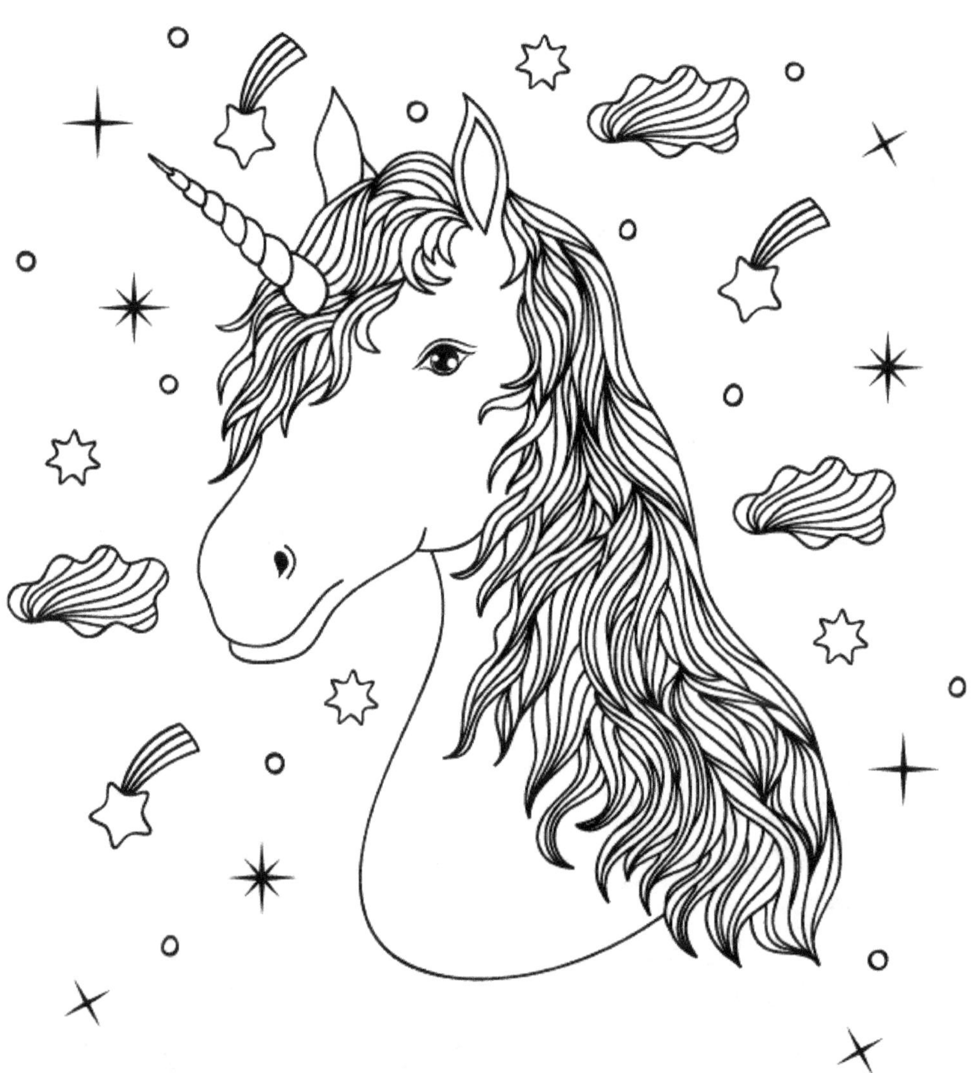

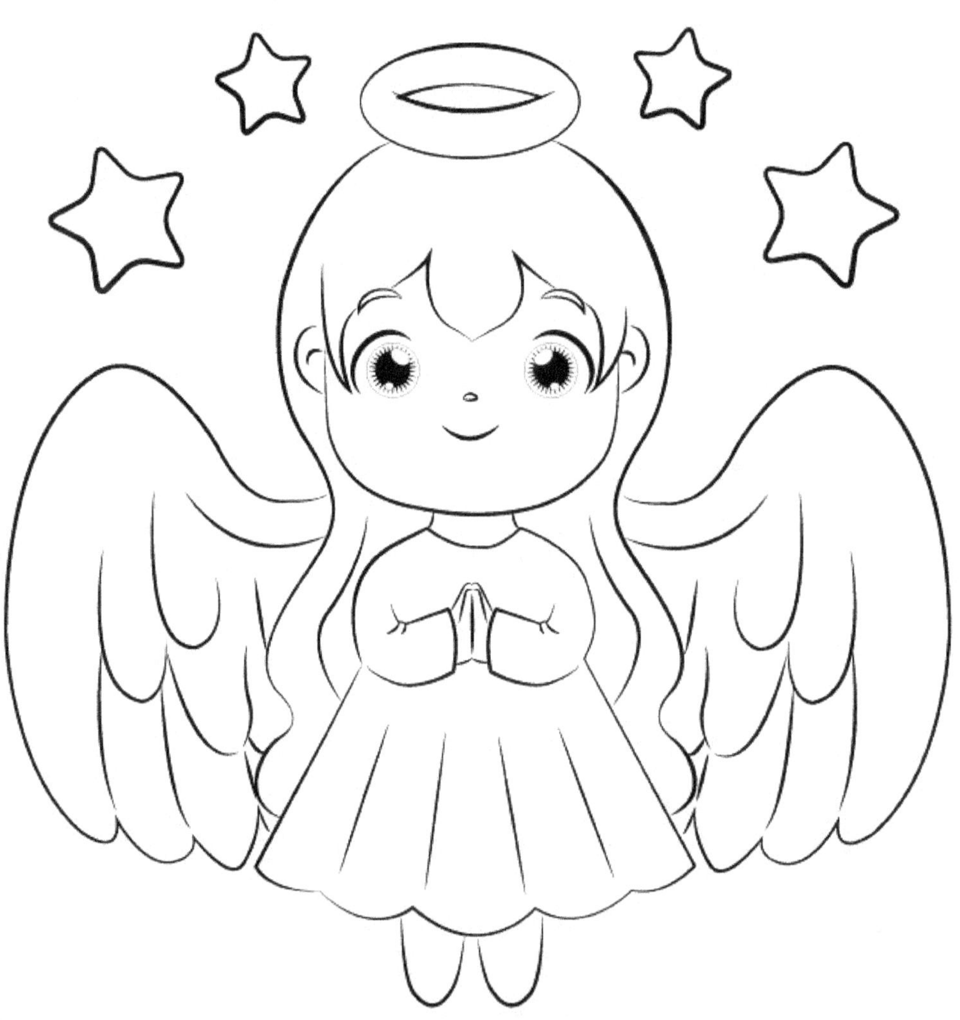

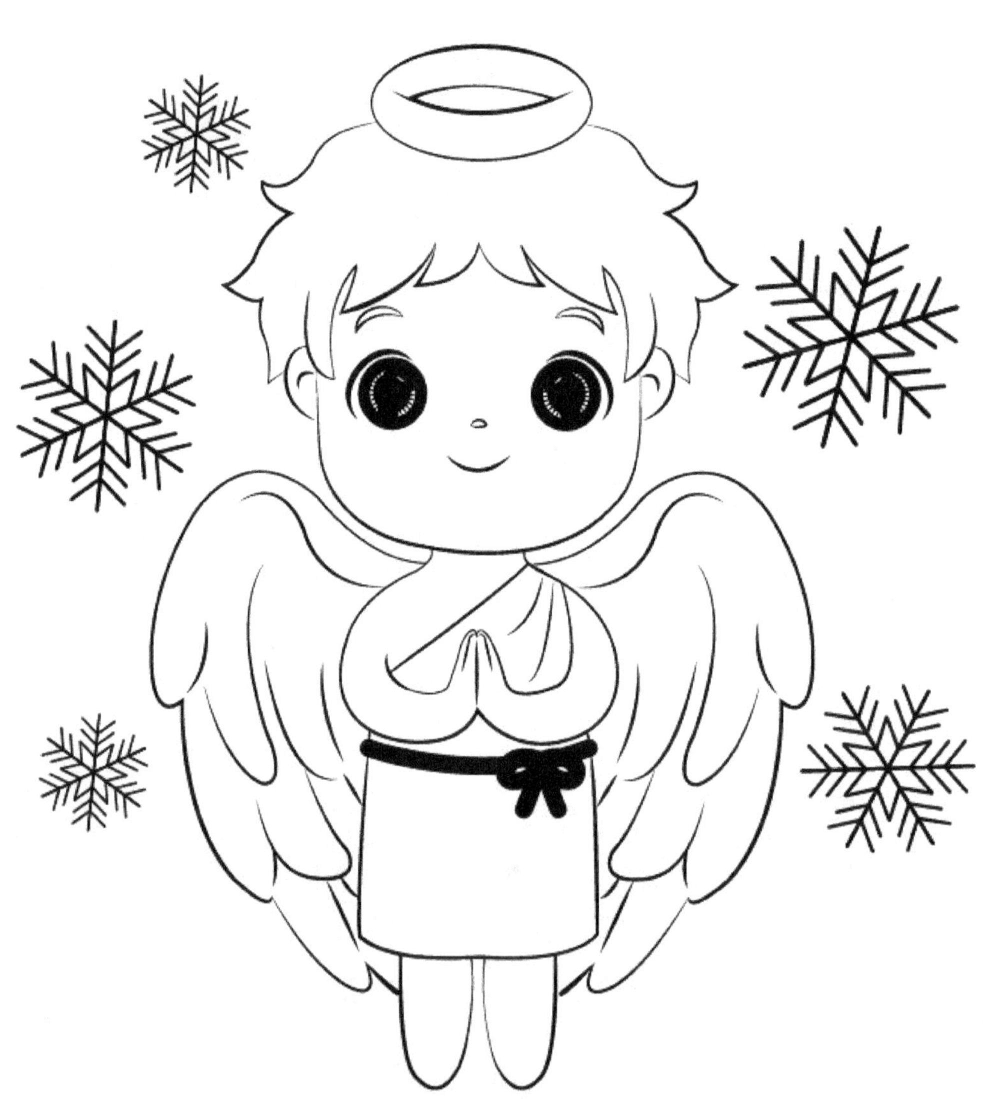

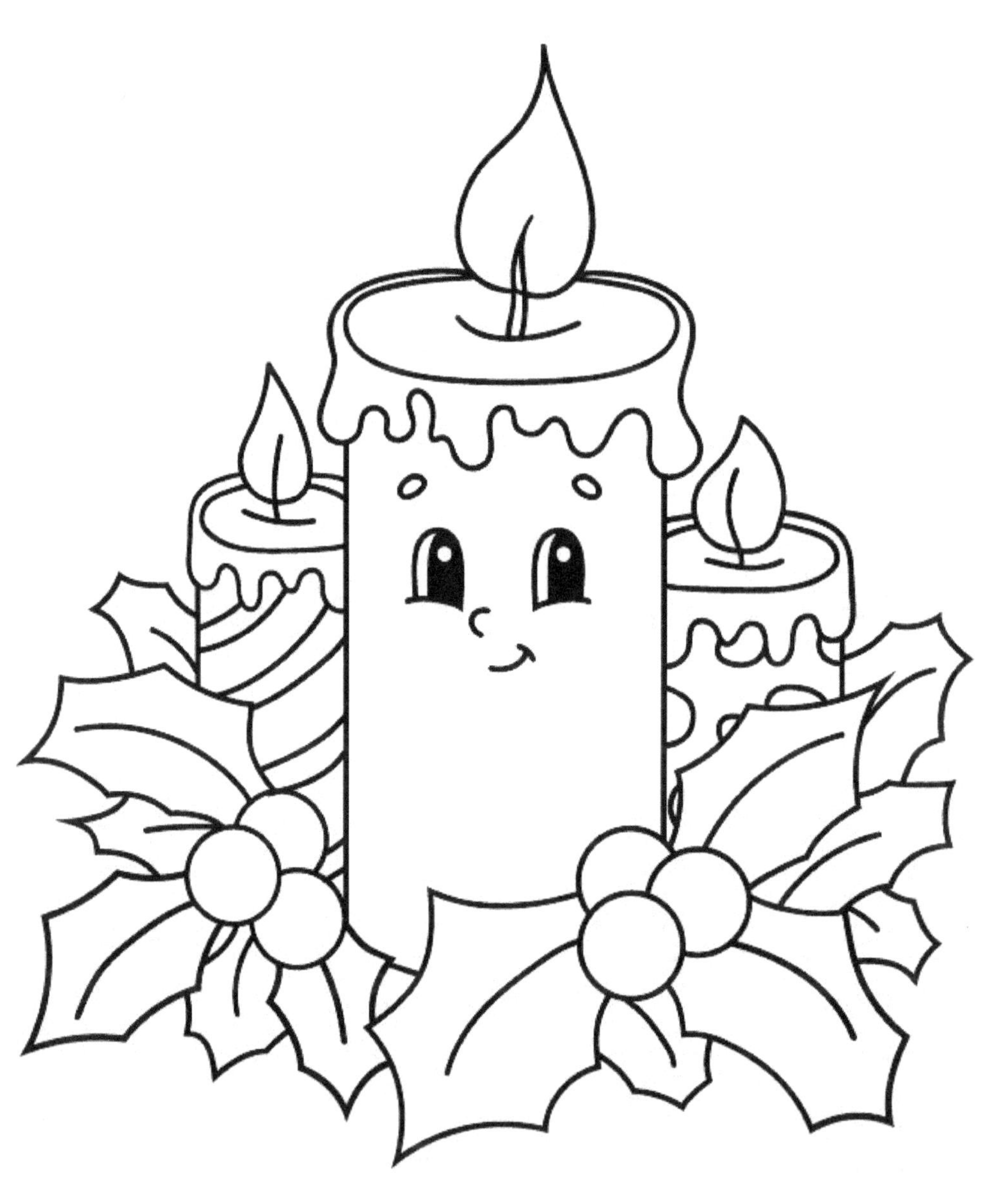

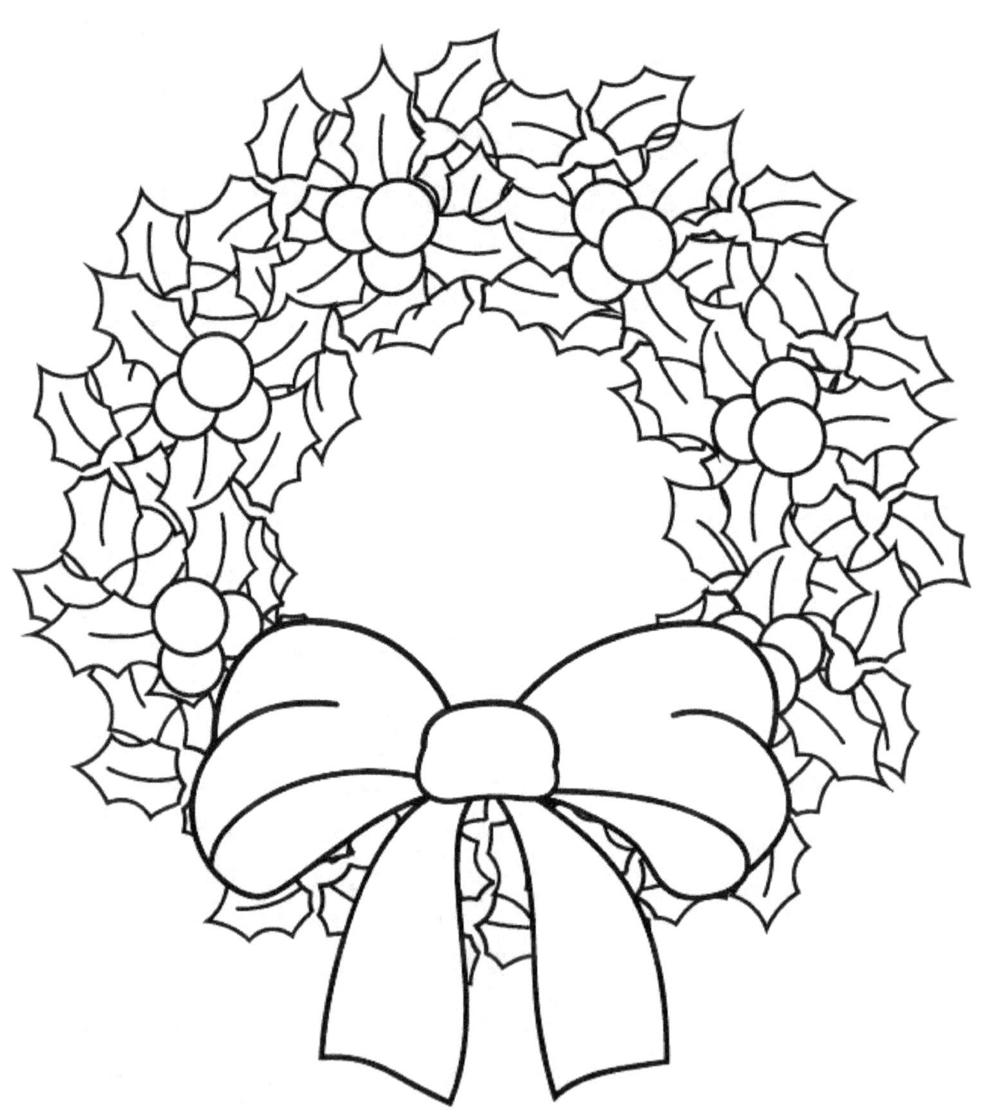

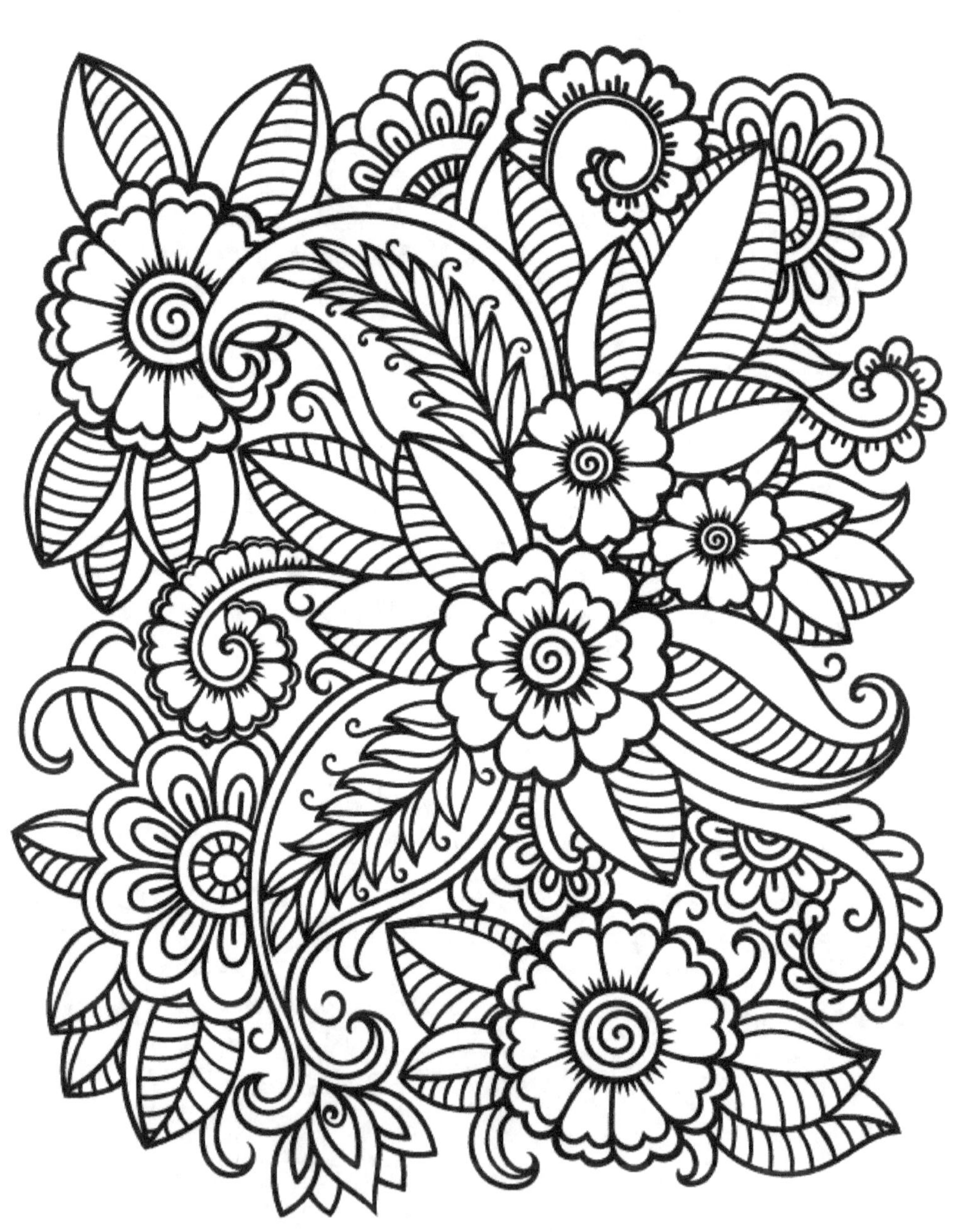

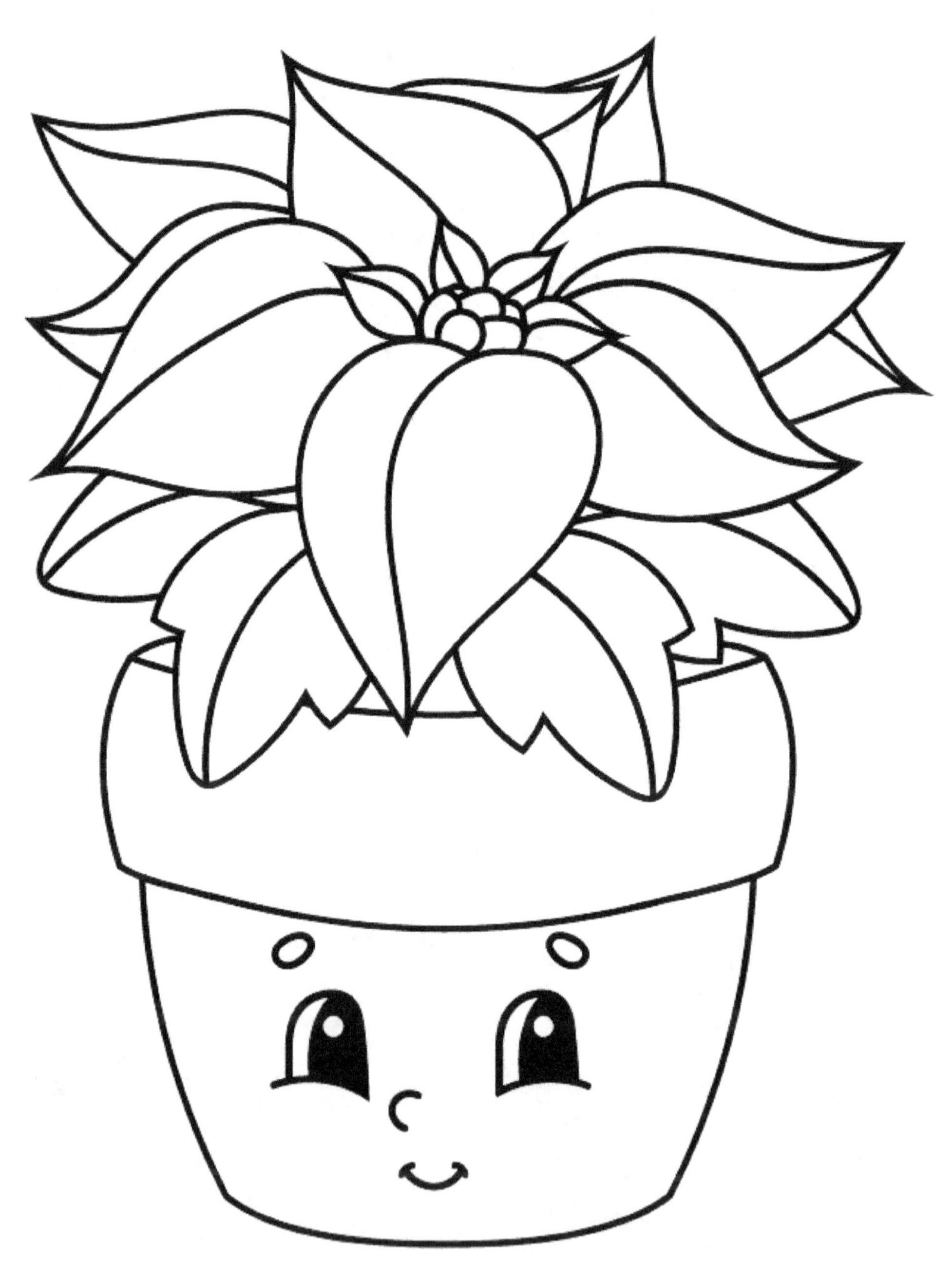

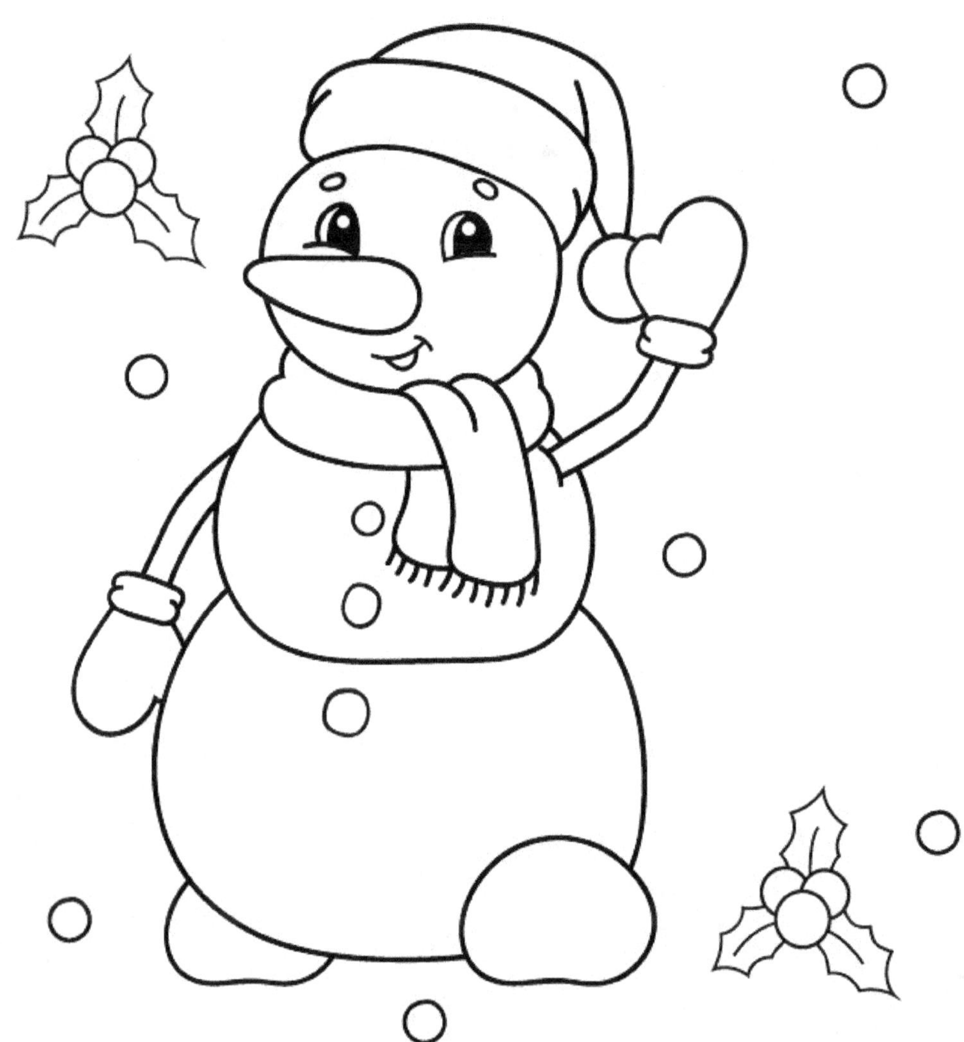

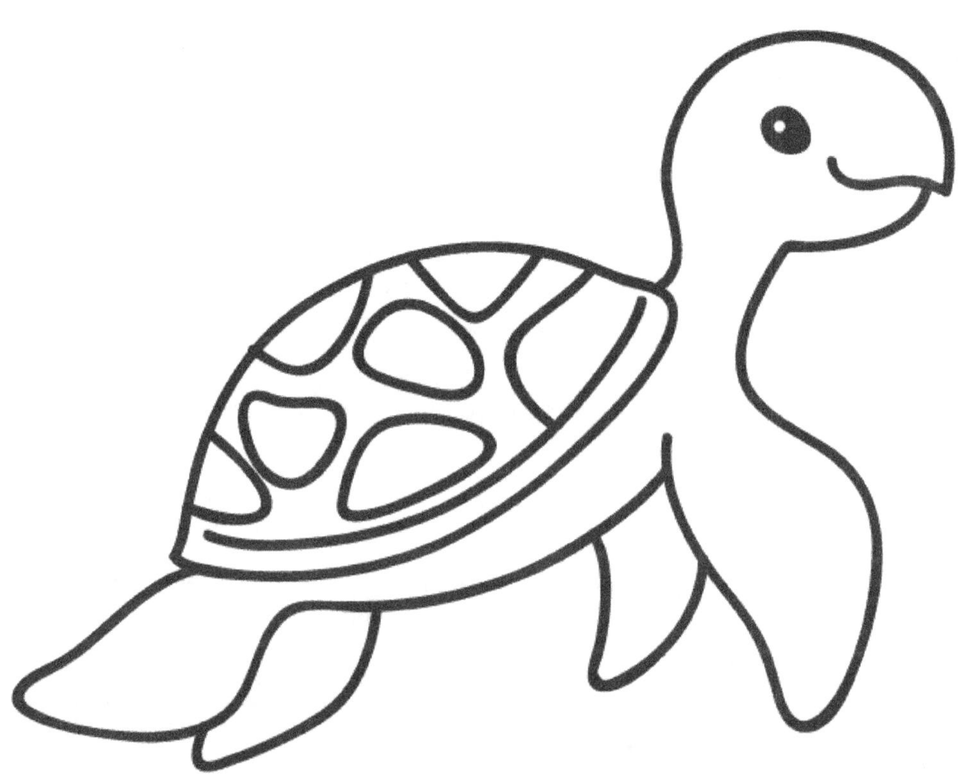

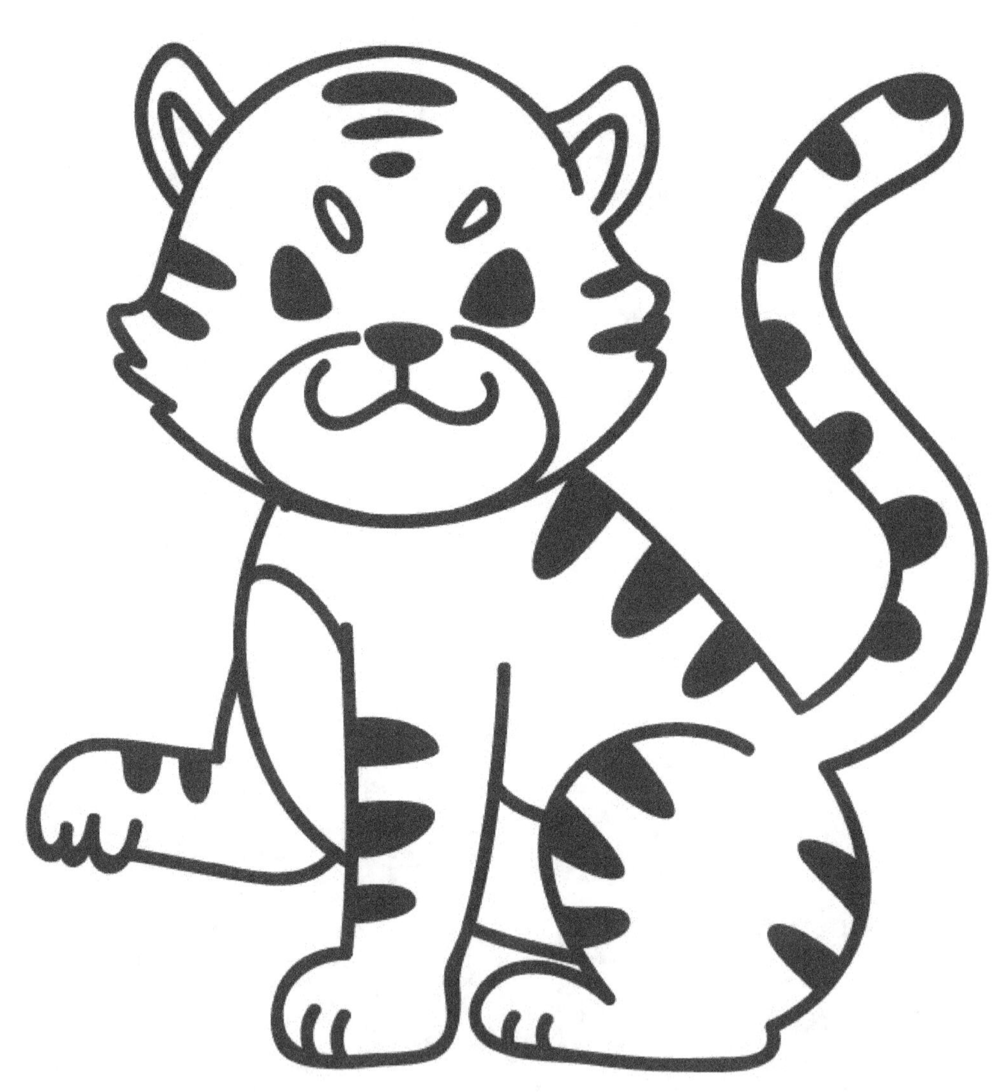

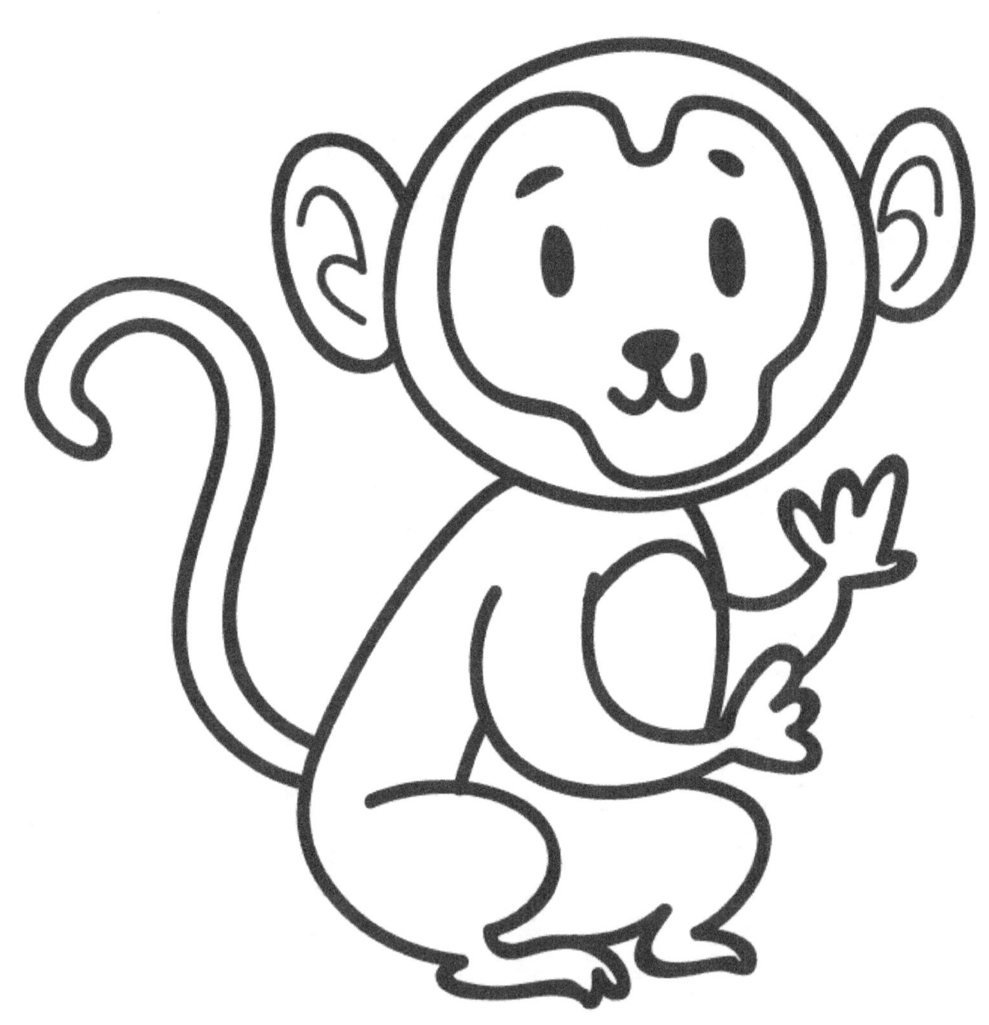

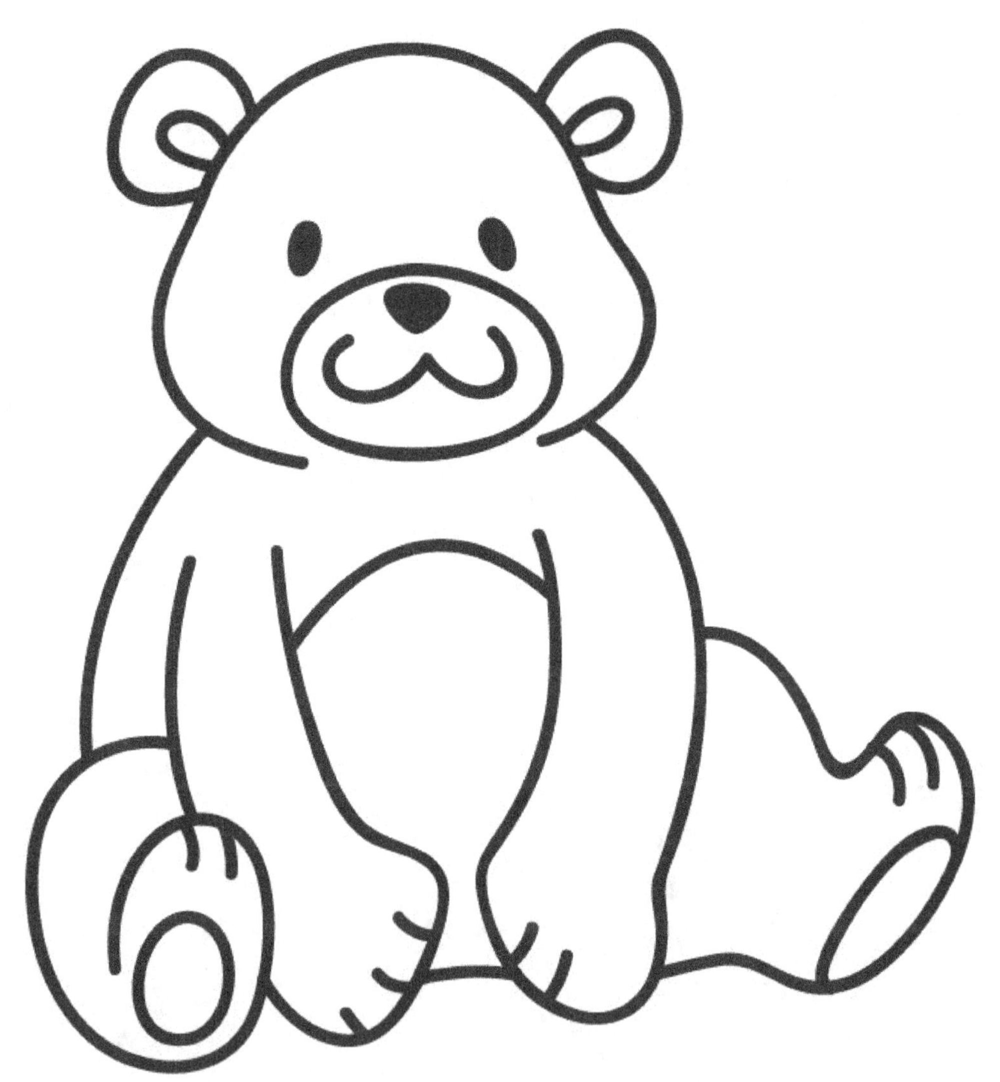

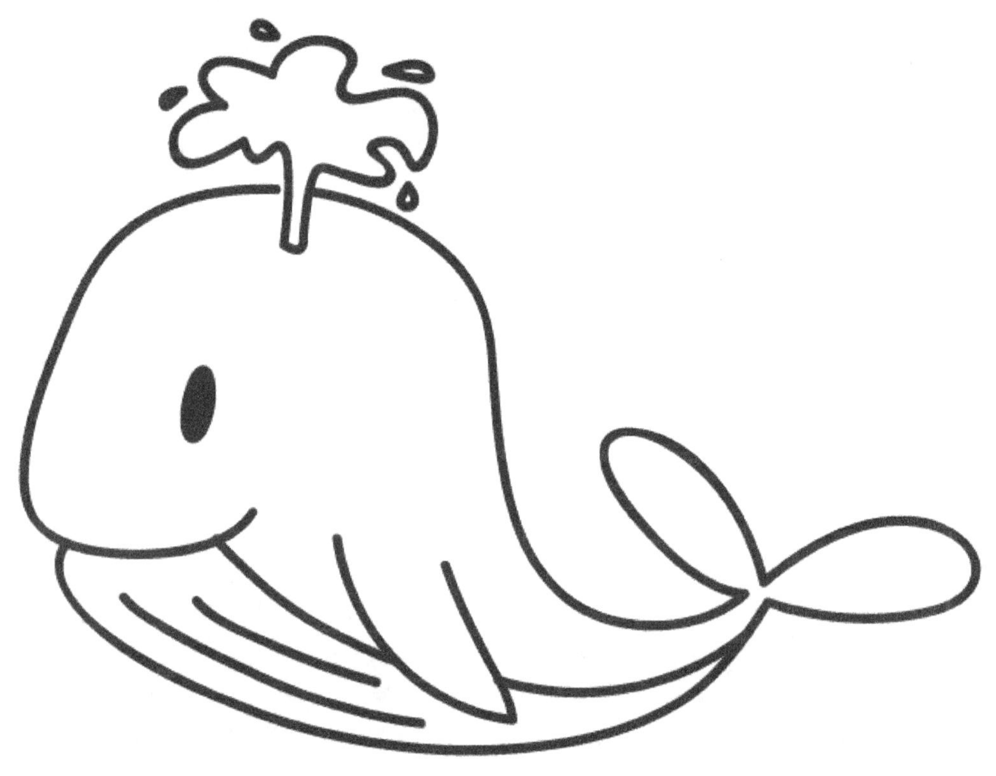

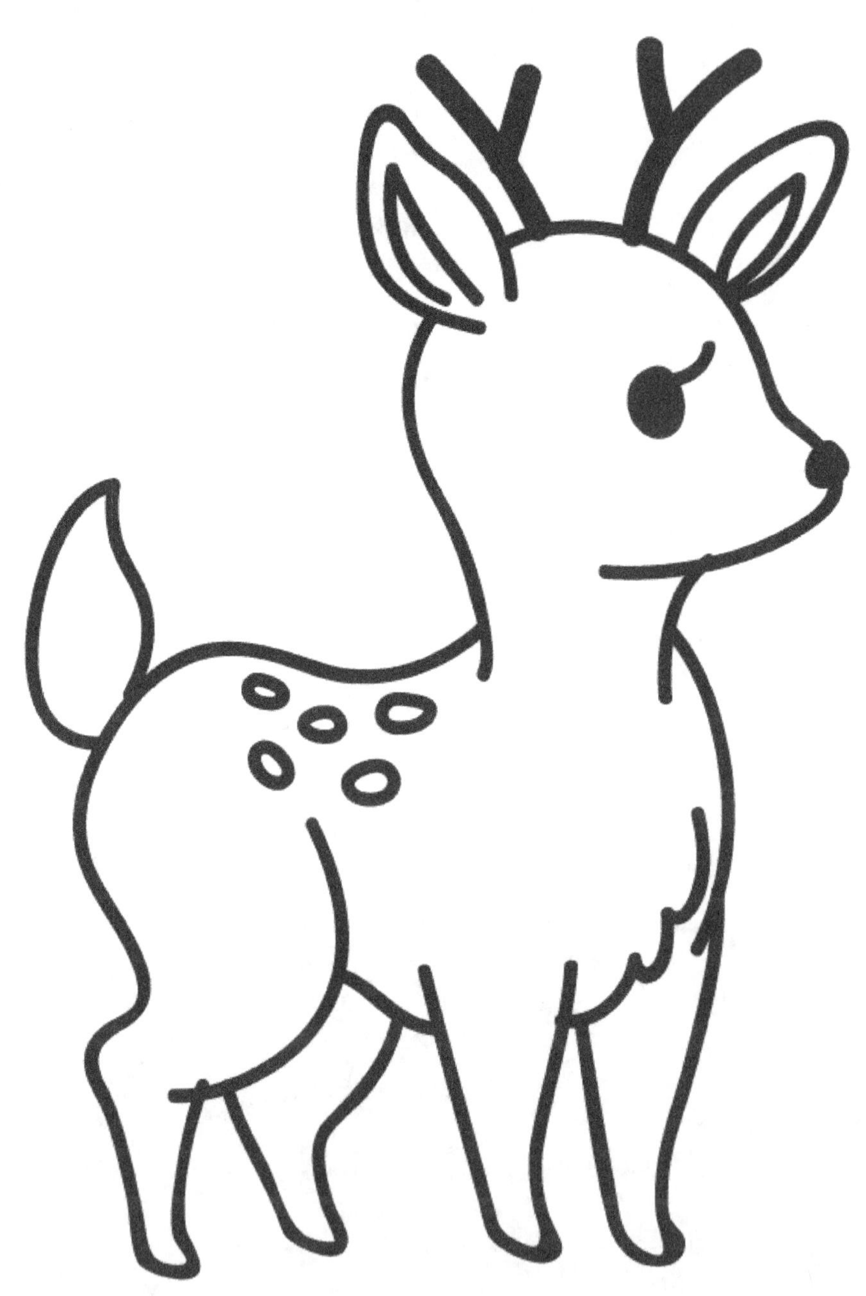

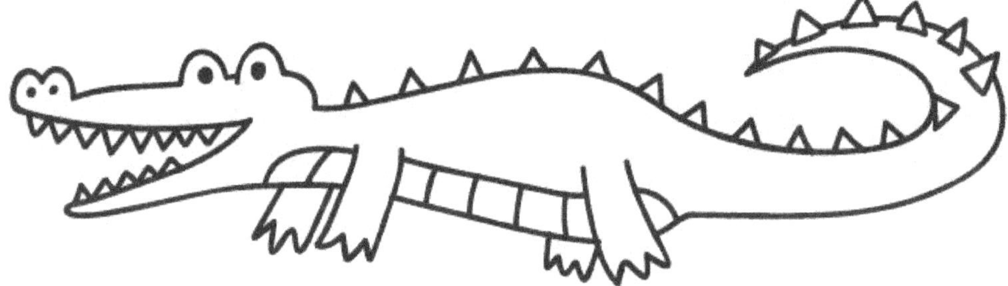

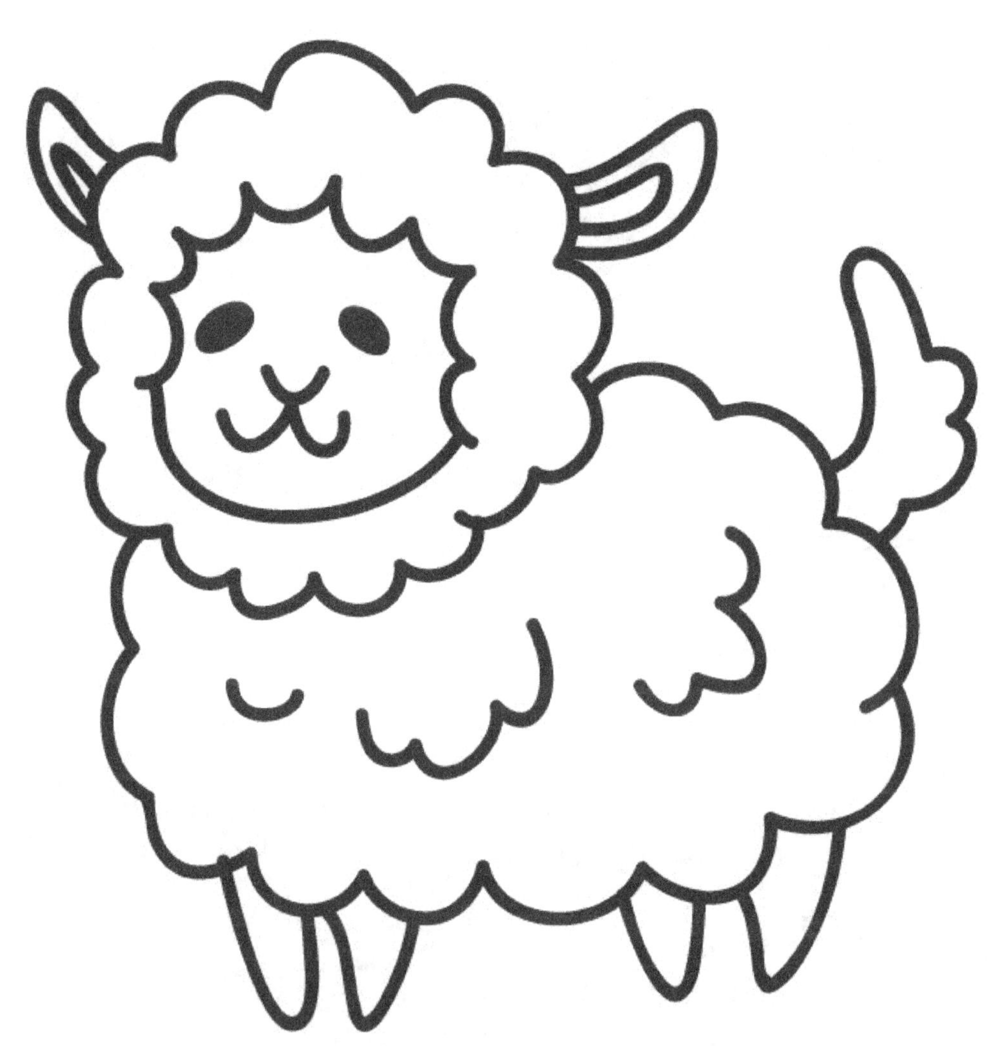

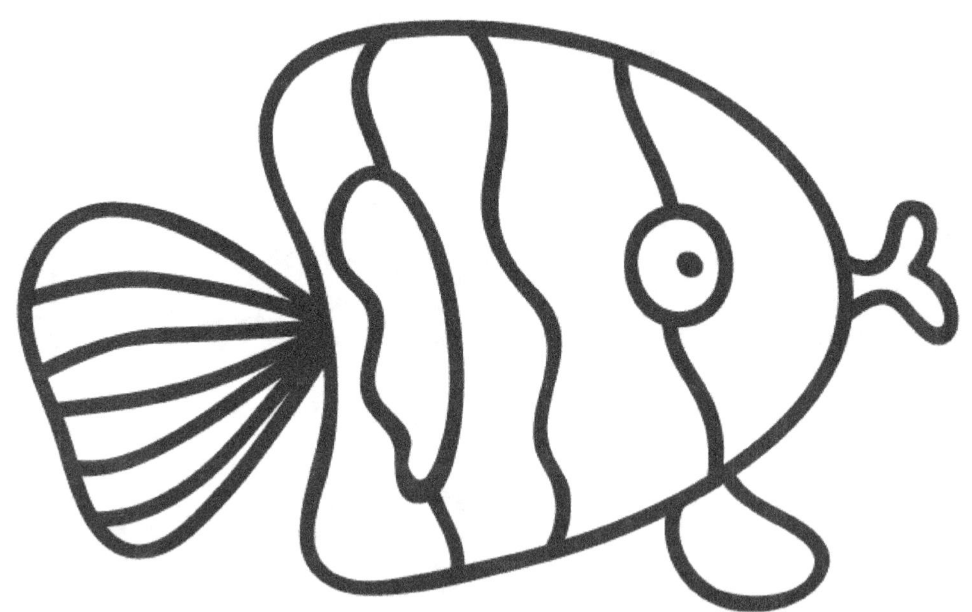

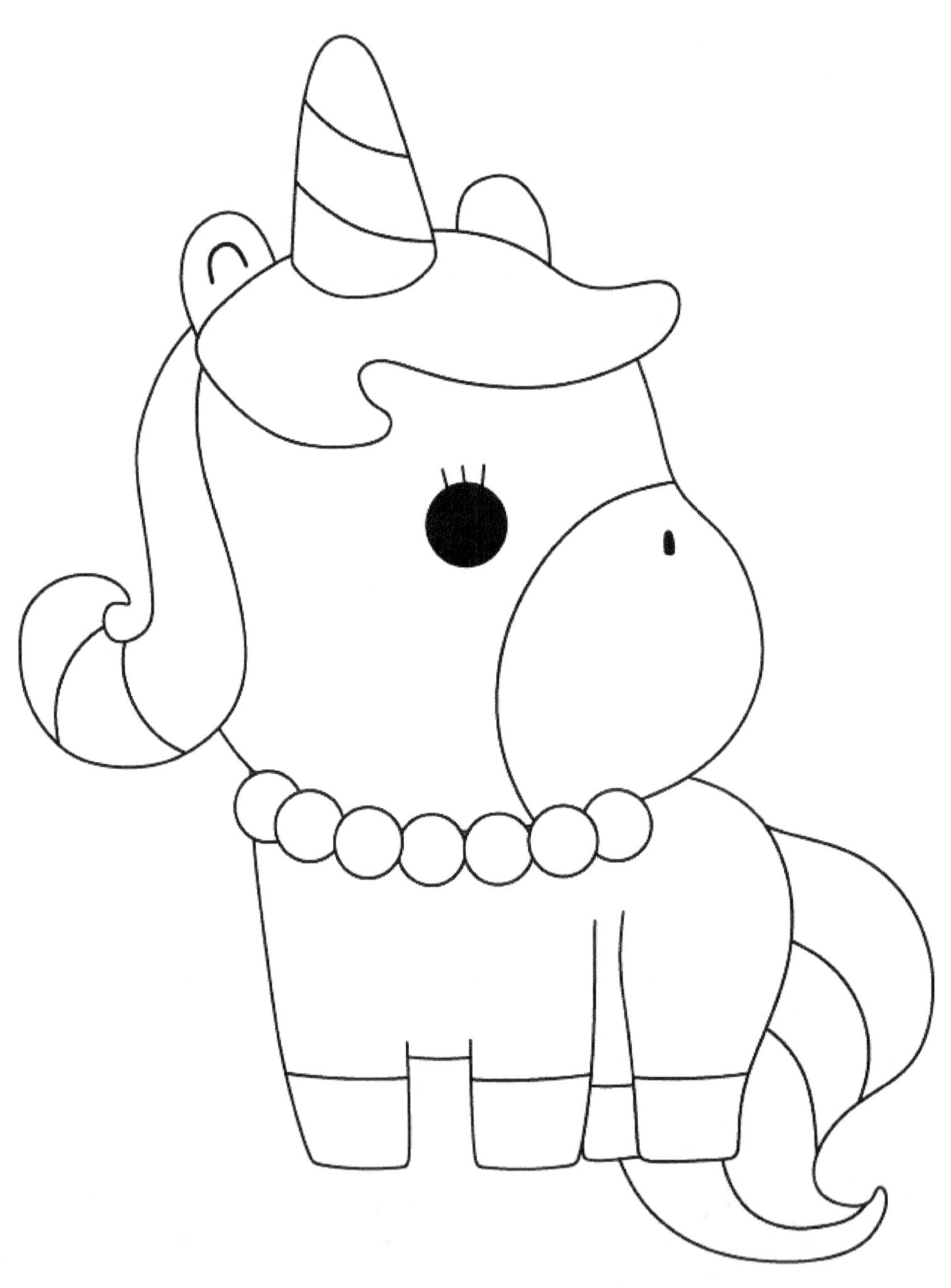

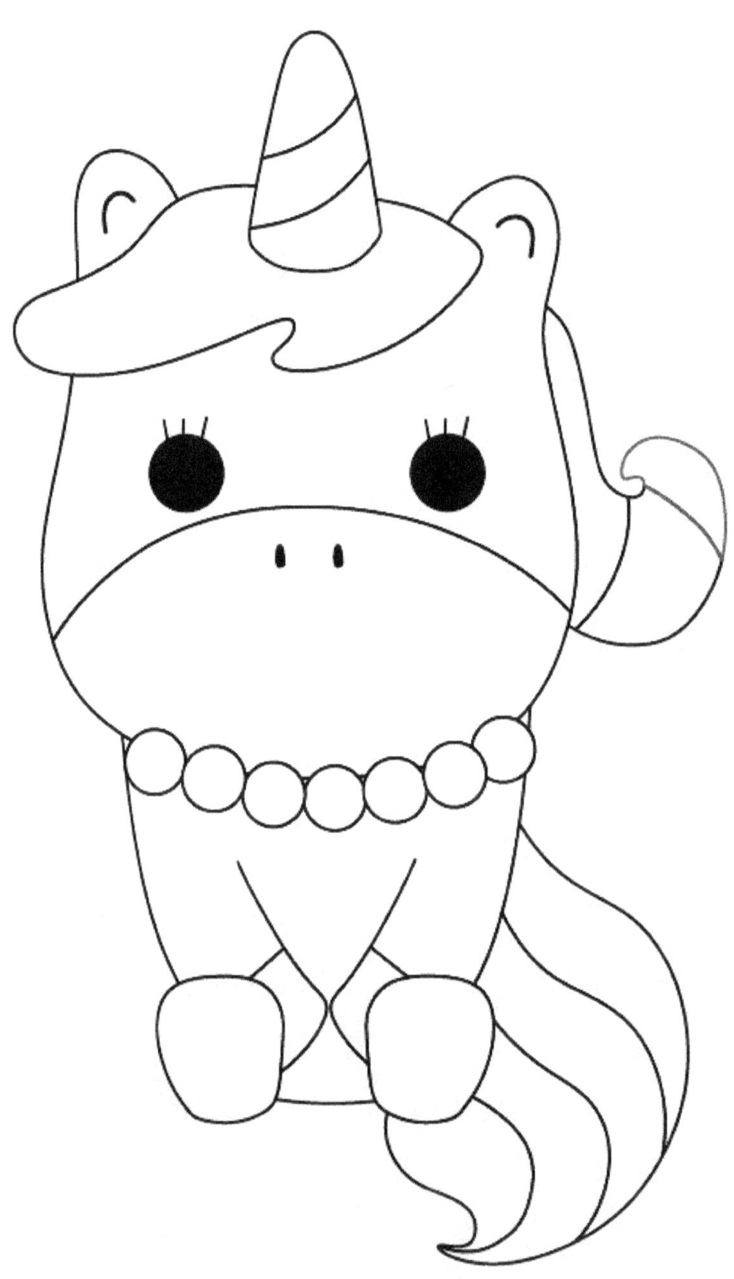

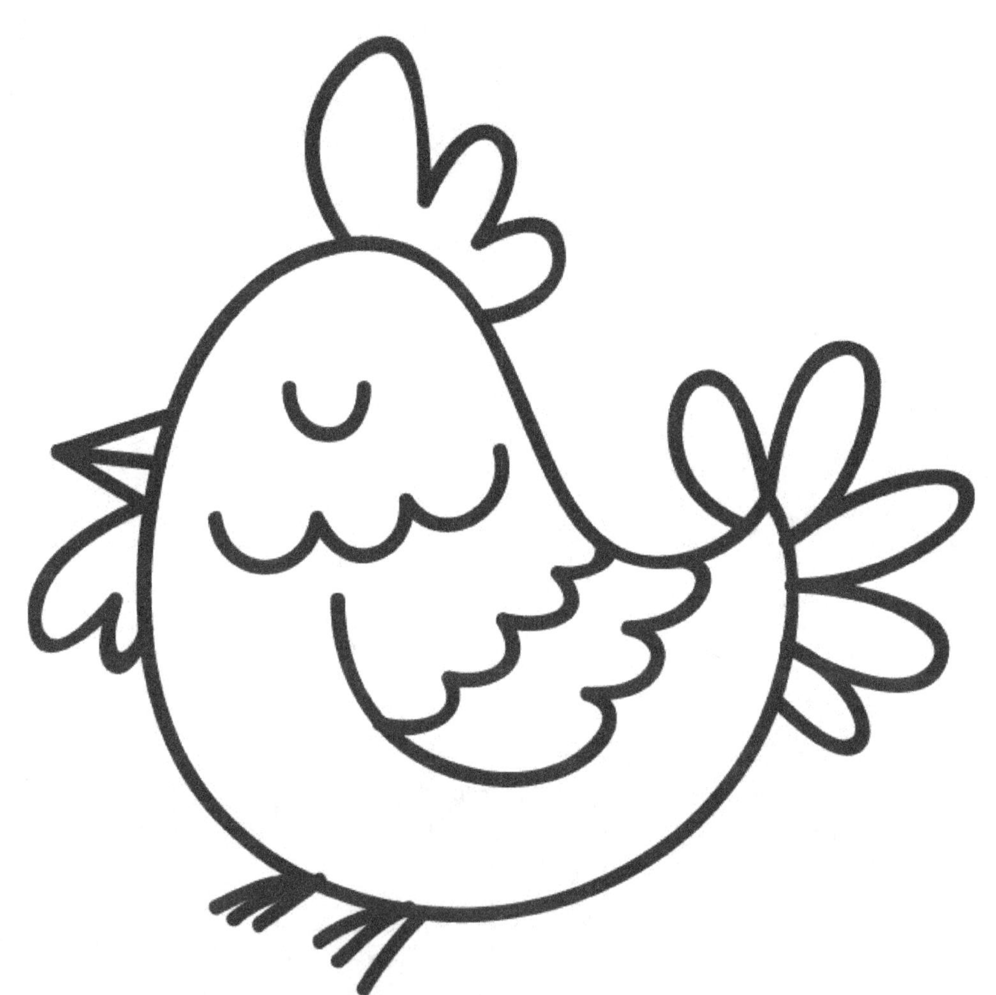

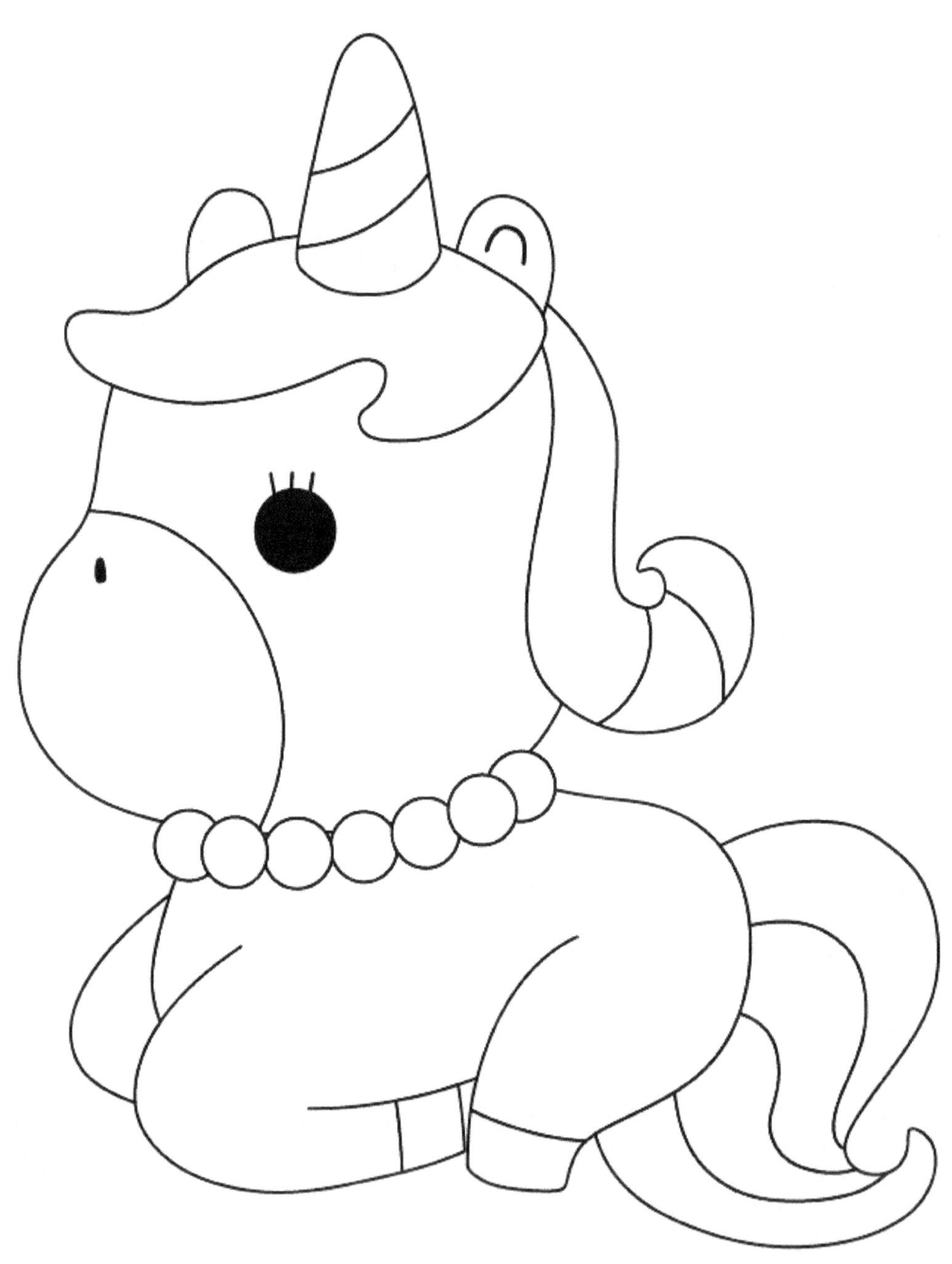

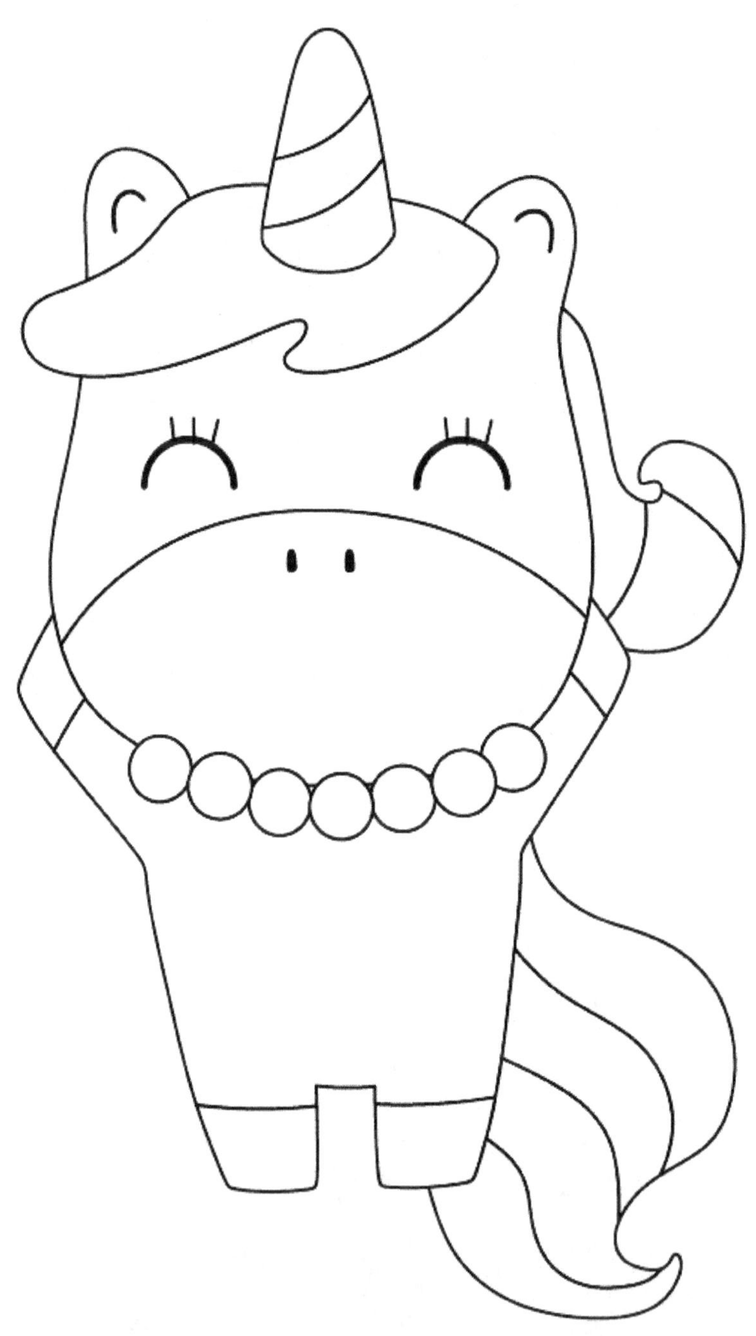

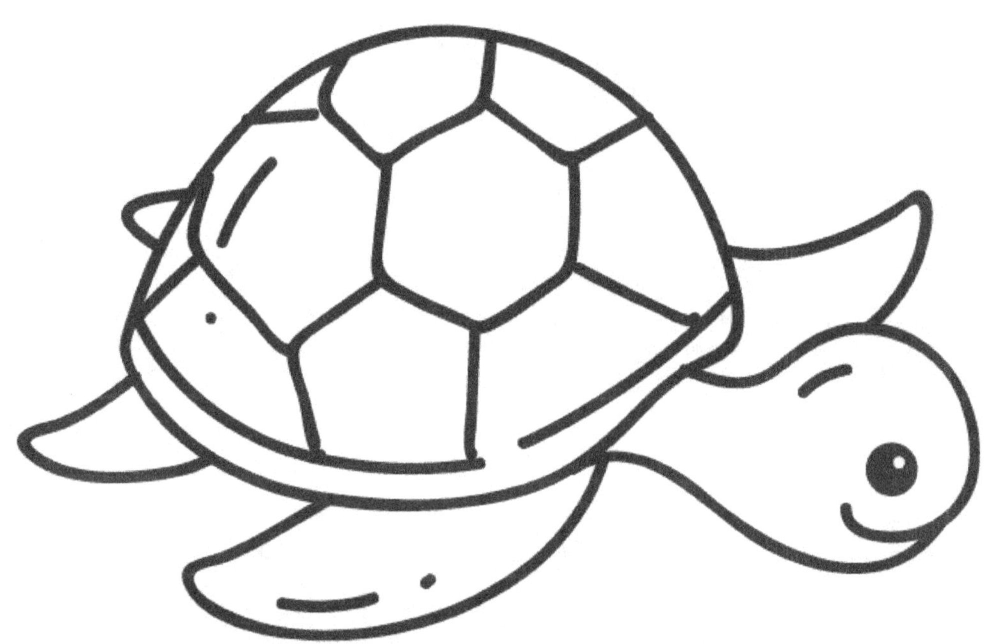

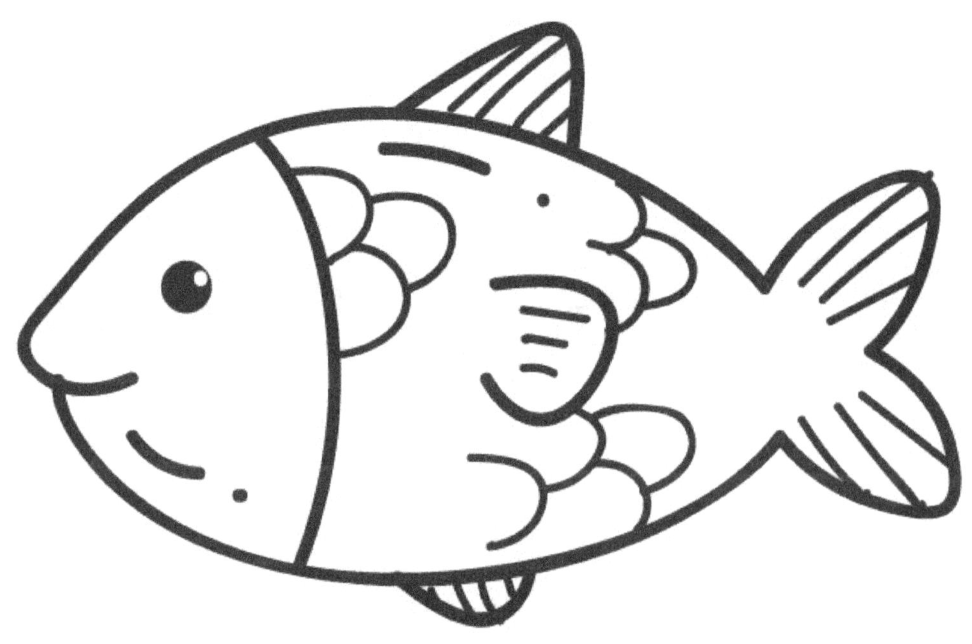

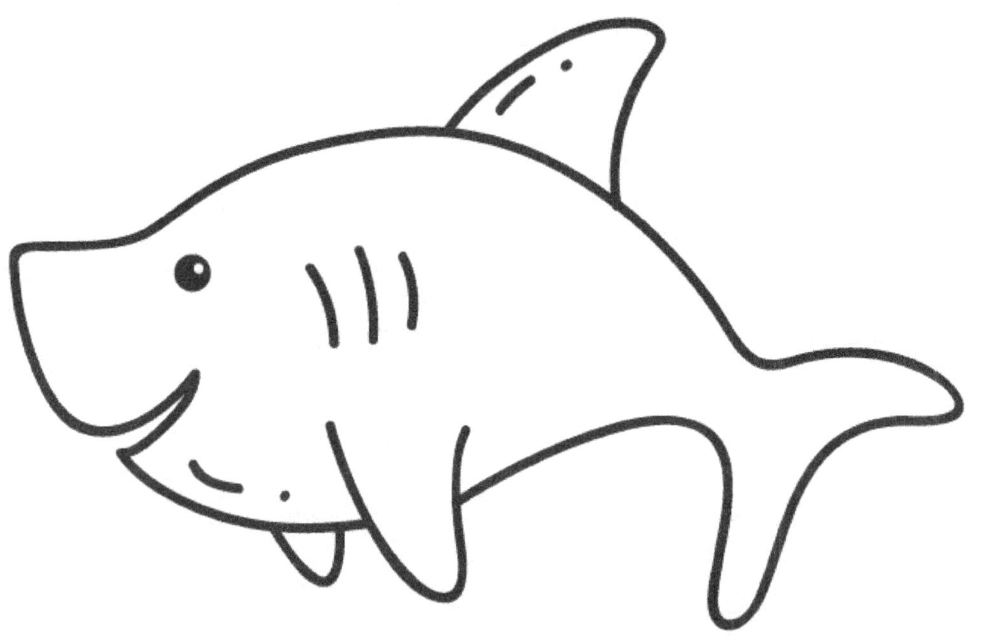

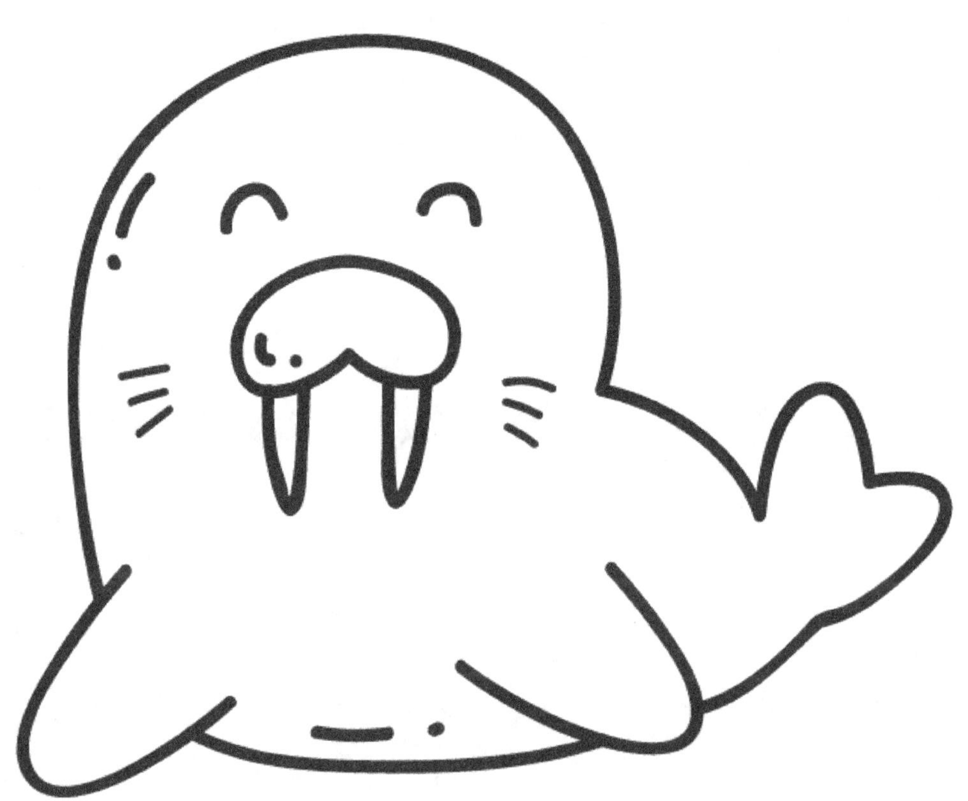

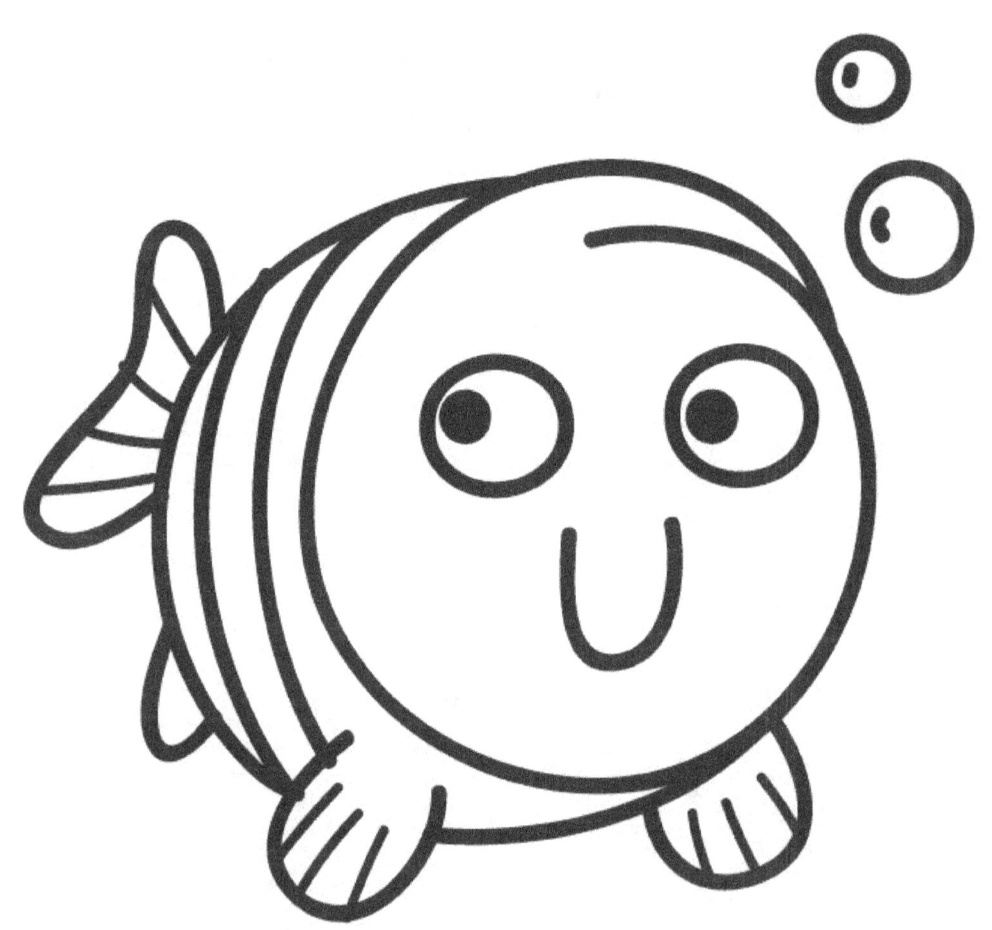

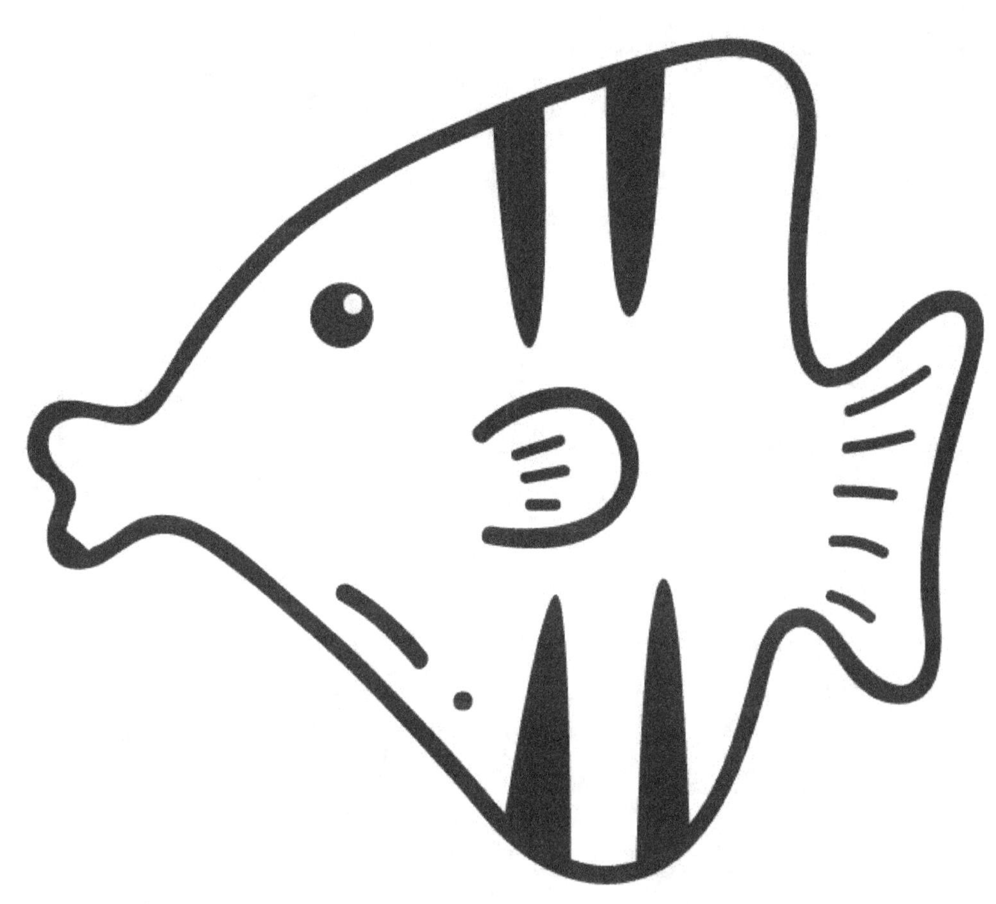

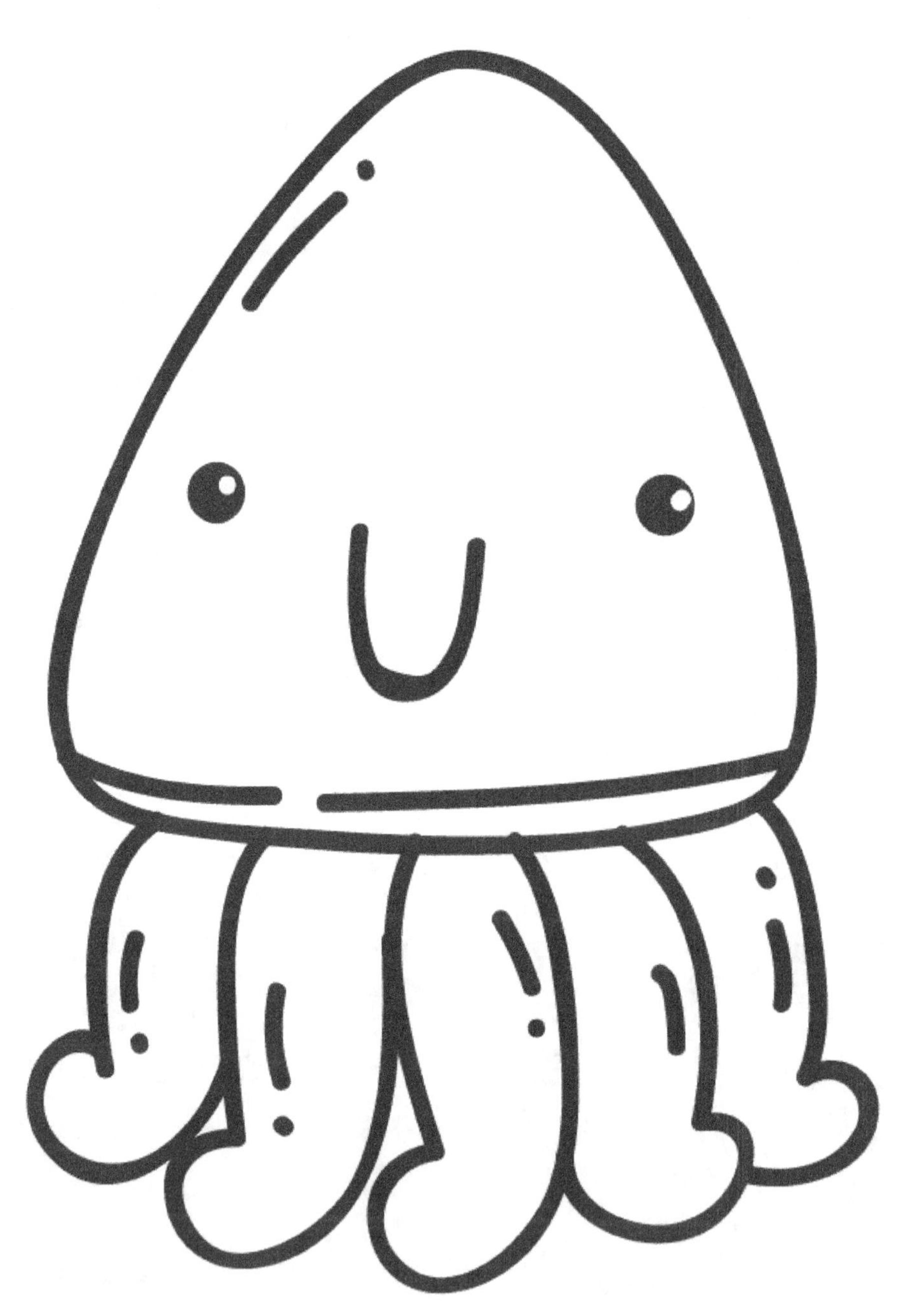

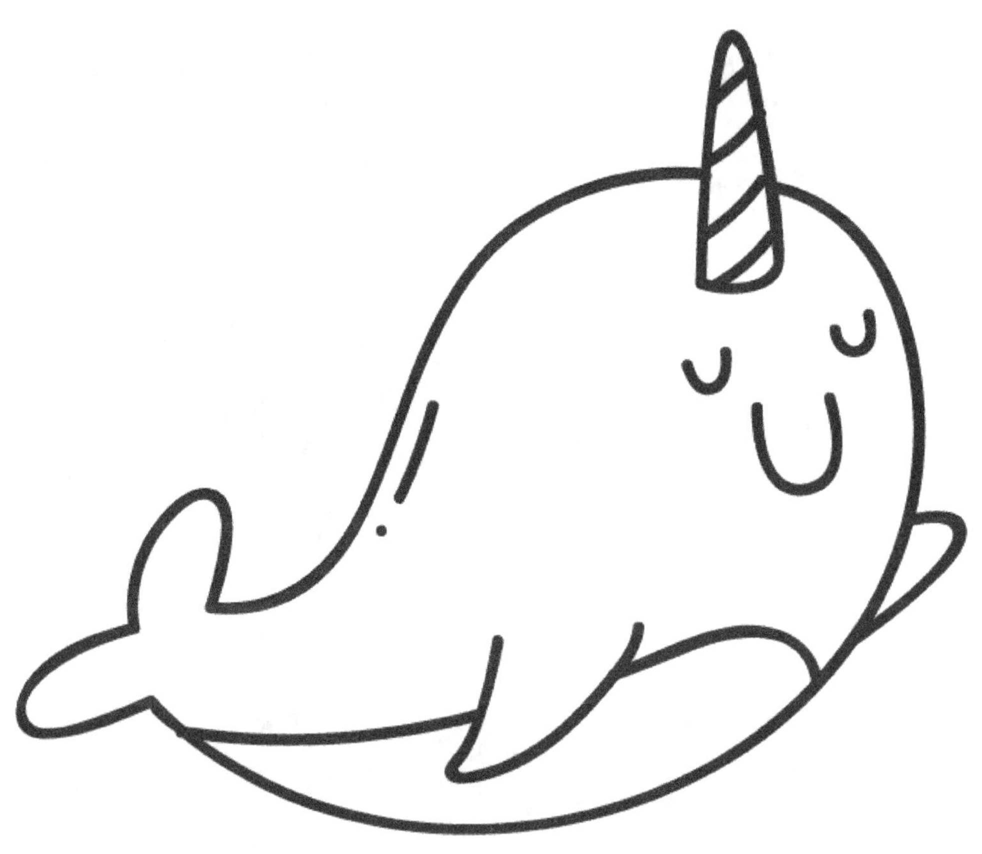

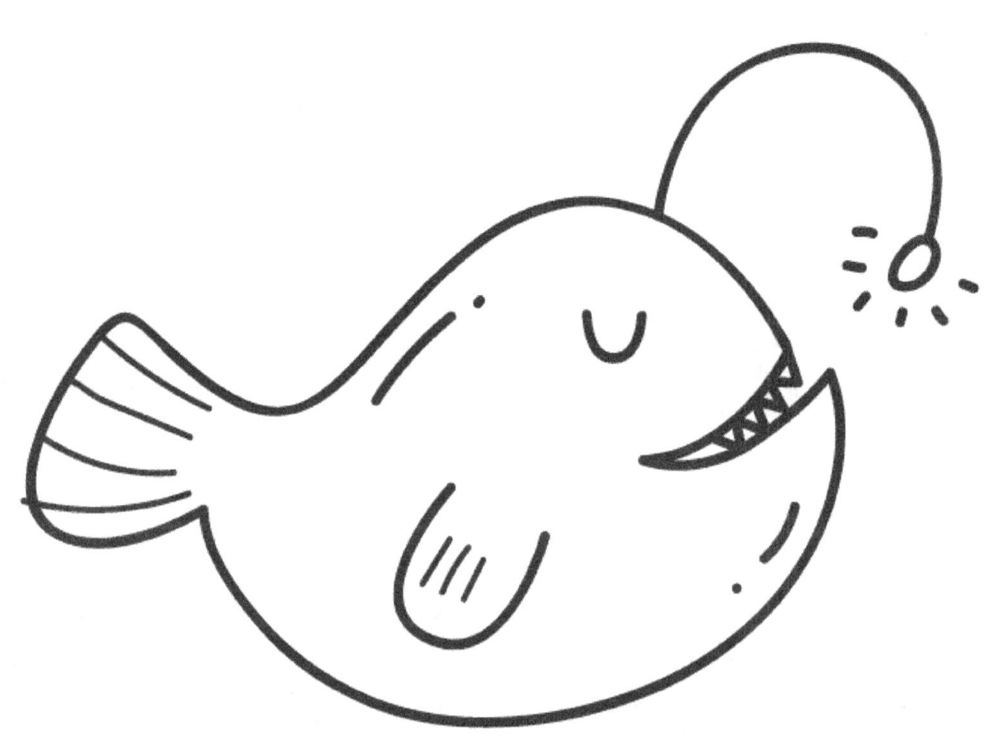